LINDA GOOD

ARIES

Also by Linda Goodman in Pan Books

Linda Goodman's Love Signs

Linda Goodman's Sun Signs
(one volume)

Linda Goodman's Star Signs

LINDA GOODMAN'S SUN SIGNS

ARIES
21 March to 20 April

Pan Books

London, Sydney and Auckland

First published in Great Britain 1970 by
George G. Harrap & Co Ltd
as part of a volume containing all twelve Sun signs
This edition published 1989 by Pan Books Ltd,
Cavaye Place, London SW10 9PG

10 9 8 7 6 5 4 3 2 1

© Linda Goodman 1968, 1989

ISBN 0 330 31000 3

Phototypeset by Input Typesetting Ltd, London
Printed and bound in Great Britain by Richard Clay Ltd, Bungay, Suffolk

For Mike Todd
the Gemini
who really knew the people he knew
and for Melissa Anne
the Pisces
to keep a promise . . .
Thus grew the tale of Wonderland:
Thus slowly, one by one,
Its quaint events were hammered out –
And now the tale is done . . .

Acknowledgement

I would like to express my grateful thanks for the help and advice given me by my friend and teacher, astrologer Lloyd Cope, a Virgo. Without his encouragement and faith, these books might have remained just another Aries dream.

The verses used throughout the text have been taken from the works of Lewis Carroll.

The term 'Sun sign' means that, if you are, for example, a Gemini, the Sun was in the zone of the zodiac called Gemini when you were born, approximately between 21 May and 21 June, inclusive. You'll find that the dates covering Sun sign periods are slightly different, depending on which astrology book you read. Most astrologers don't wish to confuse the layman with the information that the Sun changes signs in the morning, afternoon or evening of a particular day. It's all very nice and neat and easy to pretend each new sign begins precisely at midnight. But it doesn't. For example, except for leap year variations, the Sun, for the last several decades as well as at the present, both leaves Aries and enters Taurus sometime on 20 April. It's important to know that 20 April contains both signs. Otherwise, you might go around all your life thinking you're a Taurus when you're really an Aries. Remember that if you were born on the *first* or the *last* day of any of the Sun sign periods, you'll have to know the exact time and the longitude and latitude of your birth to judge whether or not the Sun had changed signs by that hour.

Contents

Foreword

How to understand Sun signs

A tale begun in other days,
When summer suns were glowing –
A simple chime, that served to time
The rhythm of our rowing –

Some day, you will doubtless want the complete details of your personal natal chart. Meanwhile, you can be sure that studying your Sun sign is an important first step. However, studying your Sun sign shouldn't be confused with studying the predictions based on your Sun sign alone in magazines and newspapers. They may hit you with impressive accuracy more often than they miss, but they're far from being infallible. Only a natal chart calculated for the exact hour and minute of your birth can be completely dependable in such a specialized area.

On the other hand, don't believe the common accusation that these predictions are 'just a bunch of general phrases that can be scrambled around to fit anybody'. That's equally untrue. The predictions (indications would be a better word) apply as they are printed, to the Taurus or Pisces or Virgo person individually. They don't apply helter-skelter to any of the twelve Sun signs. They are written by competent professionals and based on mathematical calculations of the aspects formed between your natal Sun and the planets moving overhead, and they give you a fair degree of accuracy, as far as they go. The fact that they're not based on the *exact degree* of your natal

Sun, nor on the additional aspects from the other eight planets in your natal chart, plus your natal Moon, is what creates the flaw. Still, they can be interesting and helpful, if allowances are made for the discrepancies.

The Sun is the most powerful of all the stellar bodies. It colours the personality so strongly that an amazingly accurate picture can be given of the individual who was born when it was exercising its power through the known and predictable influences of a certain astrological sign. These electromagnetic vibrations (for want of a better term in the present stage of research) will continue to stamp that person with the characteristics of his Sun sign as he goes through life. The Sun isn't the only factor in analysing human behaviour and traits, but it's easily the most important single consideration.

Some astrologers feel that a book about Sun signs is a generalization comparable to lumping together all the Polish, Irish, Chinese, Negro, Italian and Jewish people – or like lumping all butchers, bakers, candlestick makers, merchants or Indian chiefs. Though I respect their feelings, I can't agree with them. True, Sun signs can be misleading if they're used with the wrong attitude. But in the absence of a natal chart, they're far ahead of any other known quick, reliable method of analysing people and learning to understand human nature.

An individual's Sun sign will be approximately eighty per cent accurate, sometimes up to ninety per cent. Isn't that far better than zero knowledge? That extra ten or twenty per cent is, of course, most important and must be considered. But if you know a person's Sun sign, you're substantially better informed than those who know nothing about him at all. There are no pitfalls in applying Sun sign knowledge when it's done with discretion. Just plant an imaginary policeman in your mind to keep warning you that you might be off by that ten or twenty per cent, and you can use them with confidence.

What is a Sun sign? A particular zone of the zodiac – Aries, Taurus, Gemini, etc. – in which the Sun was located at the moment you drew your first breath, an exact position taken from a set of tables called an ephemeris, calculated by astronomers. As printed out in the note to the reader that precedes the Table of Contents, if you were born on the *first* or the *last* day of any Sun sign period, you'll have to know your exact birth time and the longitude and latitude of your birth place to judge whether or not the Sun had changed signs by that hour. In other words, the dates which begin and end the Sun sign periods in this or any astrology book are approximate, and this is most important to remember. These two days are called the cusps, and don't let them confuse you. Some astrologers even give them a longer period. But either way there's been entirely too much stress laid on them for the layman. No matter what you've heard, if the Sun was in Aries when you were born, it was in Aries, however near it may be to the cusp, and that's that. The influences which may be impressed on your personality from the sign preceding or following Aries will never blot out your Arian characteristics enough to turn you into a Piscean or an Aquarian. Nothing can dim the brilliance of the Sun, while it's actually in a sign, and the variations you get from being born on a cusp are never strong enough to substantially alter your basic Sun sign personality. The important thing is to establish through your birth hour that you were definitely born within the cusps. Make a small allowance for them, and then forget it.

What is a natal chart? You can think of it as a photograph of the exact position of all the planets in the sky at the moment of your birth, formed by precise mathematical calculation. In addition to the Sun and Moon (the two luminaries), there are eight planets, all of which influence your life, according to the signs they were in when you were born, their distance from each other by degrees (aspects) and their exact location.

If you were born on 9 April, you're an Arian, of course, because the Sun was in Aries, and about eight out of every ten Arian traits will show in your character. However, the Moon, ruling your emotions, might have been in Gemini, colouring your emotional attitudes with Gemini qualities. Mercury, ruling the mind, could have been in Scorpio, so your mental processes would often be Scorpion in nature. Mars, ruling your speech and movements, among other things, could have been in Taurus, so you would speak rather slowly, like a Taurean. Venus might have been in Capricorn, giving you an essentially Capricorn attitude in love, artistic and creative matters – and so on with the other planets. Yet, none of these placements will totally erase the basic qualities of your Arian Sun. They simply refine the details of your complex personality.

There are other factors to consider if you're to be one hundred per cent correctly analysed. For one thing, the aspects formed between the planets and the luminaries at your birth can modify their positions in the signs. But the most important consideration is your ascendant – the sign rising on the eastern horizon when you took your first breath – and its exact degree. Your ascendant greatly modifies the personal appearance (though your Sun sign has a lot to say about that, too) and it forms your true inner nature, upon which the motivations of your Sun sign are based. If your ascendant is Aquarius, for example, you may have strong Aquarian leanings, and wonder why the descriptions of your Arian Sun sign don't include all of your idiosyncrasies and secret longings. The two most important positions in any natal chart, after the Sun sign, are the ascendant and the Moon sign.

You'll find it interesting to obtain your ascendant from an astrologer (which can be done quickly over the telephone), and then read the description for that sign, along with your regular Sun sign. You'll find that the two of them blended make up your total personality to a remarkable degree. A third blending of your Moon sign with the other two will give you an even more complete picture.

Next, the houses of the horoscope must be considered. These are mathematically computed locations in the natal chart which have influence over different areas of your life. There are twelve of them, one for each sign. The first house is always ruled by the sign on your ascendant, and so on, in counter-clockwise order around the circle which forms the horoscope. The astrologer who has carefully calculated your natal chart, based on the exact time of your birth and its geographical location, must interpret the meaning of each sign's influence on these houses – or locations – also taking into consideration the planets which fall into their specified areas. Blending all the foregoing factors in analysing your character, your potential, and the indications of your past and future mistakes and possibilities (which are based on the aspects of the progressed and transiting planets to your natal planet positions) is called the art of synthesis in astrology. That's what takes the time, talent, effort and knowledge of the astrologer. Calculating the chart itself is a relatively simple task, once certain mathematical formulas are followed.

But back to your Sun sign, because, after all, that's what this book is about. In a way, saying that you're an Arian is rather like saying you're from New York, which isn't the generalization it seems to be. Wouldn't it be fairly easy to spot a Texan in a New York bar – or a New Yorker in a Texas restaurant? Isn't there a considerable difference between a Georgian politician and a Chicago industrialist? Of course. A rather marked difference.

Imagine that you're a Texan, discussing a man who is about to arrive for a business meeting. Someone says, 'He's a New Yorker,' and immediately an image is formed. He'll probably have faster, more clipped speech than a Texan, be less warm in his personal relationships, and will want to plunge into business without too many preliminary pleasantries. He'll probably be in a hurry to get the contracts signed and catch a plane back to the east coast. He'll be sophisticated to some degree, and probably more liberal than the Texan in his politics. Why is this instant impression likely to be pretty accurate? Because the New Yorker lives a fast life in a fast city, where slow reactions may lose him the seat on the subway or the taxi in the rain. He's constantly rubbing shoulders or elbows with the famous, so he's not easily awed. He has access to the latest plays and the best museums, so it's hard for him to remain unsophisticated. Due to higher crime rates and crowded living conditions, he won't be as hospitable or as interested in his neighbours as the Texan – his personality will be somewhat cooler.

Of course, a New Yorker can be a slow-talking Taurean or a slow-moving Capricorn, but he wouldn't be quite as slow as the Texan Taurean or Capricorn, would he? Nor would a fast-thinking and acting Gemini be quite as fast if he lived in Texas as he would if he lived in New York.

It's all relative.

All right, he's a New Yorker. Now assume you discover he's Italian. Another image. He's a writer for television. A third image. He's married, with six children – and yet another dimension of the man is revealed. Therefore (although this is an analogy, and all analogies are imperfect), saying he's a New Yorker is like saying he's an Arian, for instance, and adding the further information is comparable to knowing that his Moon was in Virgo and he had a Scorpio ascendant when he was born, etc. But even without the extra knowledge, just knowing that he's a New Yorker puts you considerably ahead of those who don't know if he's from Tibet or the South Sea Islands. In the same way, even without a natal chart, just knowing a man is an Arian or a Leo can give you more understanding of him than could ever be possessed by those who don't know if they're coping with a fiery Sagittarius or an earthy Taurus.

It's true that a detailed nativity can infallibly reveal the finer nuances of character. It can indicate marked inclinations towards or against dope addiction, promiscuity, frigidity, homosexuality, multiple marriages, a disturbed childhood, alienation from or neurotic attachments to relatives, hidden talents, career and financial potential. It can show clearly tendencies to honesty or dishonesty, cruelty, violence, fears, phobias and psychic ability; plus many other strengths and weaknesses of inner character which may be latent for years, then burst forth under provocation during planetary progressions and transits which affect the natal planet positions for a temporary period of time. Susceptibility and immunity to accident and disease are revealed, secret attitudes towards drink, sex, work, religion, children, romance – and the list could go on and on. There are no secrets hidden from the accurately calculated natal chart. None except your own decision concerning how much of your individual free will you may decide to exercise.

However, in the absence of such a complete analysis, everyone can profit from a study of Sun signs, and the knowledge can make us more tolerant of one another. Once you understand how deeply ingrained certain attitudes are in people's natures, you'll become more sympathetic towards their behaviour. Learning Sun signs can help cool, poised Scorpio parents to be more patient with the quick brightness they would otherwise think was restless fidgeting in a Gemini child. It helps extroverted students understand introverted teachers, and vice versa. You'll forgive the Virgo his pickiness when you realize he was born to keep every hair straight and to untangle issues by examining each detail. It's easier to bear the carelessness of the Sagittarian when you understand he's too busy finding causes to cherish and defend to look where he's going every minute or notice whose toes he's stepping on. His frankness will cut less when you're aware of his compulsion to speak the truth, whatever the cost.

You won't be as hurt when a Capricorn doesn't 'ooh' and 'ah' over the gift you gave him, after you've remembered that he's deeply grateful, but incapable of showing his pleasure openly. His insistence on duty will chafe less when you know that he disciplines himself as severely as he does others. Putting up with the endless Libran arguments and hesitations is somehow more bearable with the Sun sign knowledge that he's only trying to be fair and reach an impartial decision. The Aquarian won't seem as rude when he roots into your private life if you stop to think he was created with an uncontrollable urge to investigate people's motives.

Once in a great while you may come across a Leo, for example, with, say, five or six planets in Pisces. The Piscean influences will obviously project themselves strongly, making his Sun sign harder to guess, since they'll greatly subdue his Leo qualities. But that will happen only rarely, and if you're completely familiar with all twelve Sun signs in detail, he can't disguise his true nature for ever. No matter how hard the fish tries to hide the lion, that Leo Sun sign will never be totally eclipsed – and you'll catch him unawares.

Never make the mistake of skimming the surface when you're trying to recognize Sun signs. Not all Capricorns are meek, not all Leos are outwardly domineering and not all Virgos are virgins. You'll find an occasional Aries with a savings account, a quiet Gemini or even a practical Pisces. But look beyond the one or two traits that threw you off. You'll catch that flashy Capricorn peeking at the social register – the shy Leo pouting over a slight to his vanity – and the rare flirtatious Virgo buying insecticide by the case, because it's cheaper. The quiet Gemini may not talk fast, but her mind can operate at jet speed. The exceptional thrifty Aries will wear a bright-red Mars coat to the bank or talk back to a rude bank clerk – and the practical Pisces secretly writes poetry or invites six orphans for dinner every Thanksgiving. No one can successfully hide his or her Sun sign from you, if you keep your eyes and ears open. Even your pet will show unmistakable Sun sign traits. Don't move the food dish of a Virgo cat to a strange spot – and never try to ignore a Leo dog.

It's fun to practise with famous people, politicians, fictional heroes and heroines. Try to guess their sign, or what sign they most represent. It sharpens your astrological wits. You can even try comic-strip characters. Good old Charlie Brown is obviously a Libran, and Lucy could only be a Sagittarius with an Aries ascendant and her Moon in Virgo. As for Snoopy, well, anyone can easily see he's an Aquarian dog, the way he wears that crazy scarf and the World War I aviator's cap, while he chases an imaginary Red Baron from the roof of his dog house. (Snoopy may also have an afflicted Neptune.) Try it yourself, and you'll have lots of fun. But what's more important, as you play the Sun sign game, you'll be learning something very serious and useful: how to recognize people's hidden dreams, secret hopes and true characters – how to understand their deepest needs – how to like them better and make them like you – how to really know the people you know. It's a happier world, and people are pretty great, when you look for the rainbows hidden inside them.

Isn't that really life's major problem? Understanding? Abraham Lincoln said it simply and clearly: 'To correct the evils, great and small, which spring from positive enmity among strangers, as nations or as individuals, is one of the highest functions of civilization.'

Start right now to study your Sun signs, use reasonable caution when you apply them, and people will wonder where you got all your new perception when you begin to unmask their real natures. In fact, understanding the twelve Sun signs will literally change your life. You're on your way to understanding people you've never even met. You'll soon feel closer to strangers, as well as to friends, and isn't that really rather wonderful?

It's nice to know you . . .

Linda Goodman

'I daresay you haven't had much practice,'
said the Queen . . .
'Why, sometimes I've believed as many as
six impossible things before breakfast.'

ARIES
the Ram

21 March to 20 April

How to Recognize Aries

They would not remember the simple rules
their friends had taught them,
that a red hot poker will burn you
if you hold it too long;
and that, if you cut your finger
very deeply with a knife,
it usually bleeds.

Have you recently met an unusually friendly person with a forceful manner, a firm handclasp and and instant smile? Get ready for a dizzy dash around the mulberry bush. You've probably just been adopted by an Aries. Especially if you found it a little tough to take the lead in the conversation.

Is he committed to some idealistic cause and angrily defending the underdog? That figures. Male or female, these people will fight what they feel is an injustice on the spot, and they're not bashful about voicing their opinions. The ram will talk back to a traffic cop or an armed gangster with equal vigour, if either one happens to annoy him. He may regret it later, but caution won't concern him in the heat of the moment. Mars people come straight to the point, with no shilly-shallying.

Aries is the first sign of the zodiac. It represents birth, as Pisces represents death and consciousness of the soul. The ram is conscious only of himself. He's the infant of the zodiac – the new-born baby – completely absorbed with his own toes and fingers. His needs come first. An infant doesn't care whether or not his parents or the neighbours are sleeping. When he's hungry or wet, he yowls in discomfort. He wants his bottle, and he wants his nappy changed *now*, and don't be poky about it. When the Aries person has an idea or something he wants to get off his mind, he'll call you at four in the morning without a qualm. Why shouldn't you be awake to listen to him? He's awake. That's all that counts. He wants something. He gets it. Like the infant, Aries is concerned with the world only as it relates to himself. But who could call the small baby truly selfish? He's perfectly willing to lavish his smiles and favours on those who satisfy his demands. It's hard to resist a baby, because he's so totally unaware that he's causing anyone the slightest inconvenience. So it is with the ram. His innocence hangs over him and mellows his aggressiveness, like the innocence of the newborn softens his egocentricity.

This disarming naïveté is also why Aries people are so fearless. The baby fears nothing and no one, until he gets burned. Even then, he'll trustingly try again, when he's forgotten the hurt. There's not a trace of cunning wile in the ram, and he'll remain this way throughout his lifetime; for ever believing with all his heart, always falling down and getting up again to try once more. Any doubts he collects along the way are immediately displaced by the next person who's kind to him, just as the baby forgets the pain of the safety pin that accidentally stuck in his leg the next time someone sprinkles the powder.

The ram can make-believe from here to tomorrow, and spin fabulous dreams, but he can't lie worth a tinker. What you see before you is what he is. There's nothing hidden or complicated about him. He's just as vulnerable as the baby, and just as helpless. When stronger, more mature people force him or take things away from him, he reacts in the only manner he knows – yelling and causing so much disturbance, that people give in just to get peace. He doesn't need delicate strategy. Lung power and self-absorbed determination suffice beautifully to allow him to get his way. Perhaps helpless is not the right word. Vulnerable, yes – but helpless, no.

It's a cinch to recognise the physical appearance of the ram. Aries people have decided features, usually sharp, seldom soft or blurred. The well-marked brows often join with the narrow bridge of the nose in forming the sign of the ram (Υ), perhaps as a warning to anyone with the silly idea of trying to stop or conquer him that those symbolic horns mean business. You may notice a mole or a scar on the head or face, a reddish cast to the hair in the sunlight, and more colour than average in the complexion. You may also sense invisible sparks shooting out in all directions. The movements will usually be quick and capable, with a mental process to match. Both the male and female rams normally have broad shoulders, and they may walk with the body slightly bent forward, leading with the head, so to speak, and almost always in a great hurry. (Often, they're in a hurry to get to a brick building to knock down, though their horns may get bent in the butting.) There's little that's graceful about the ram, unless it's his smooth way of handling a crisis (which never fails to surprise people who underestimate him). The bone structure is fine and strong, and few Aries people slump. Their posture reflects their supreme ego and self-confidence. If you see an Aries with drooping shoulders, he's probably a sheep type, who was badly hurt in the ego when he was young. It may take him some time to recover, if the wounds went deep, but he'll

straighten up someday. You can count on it. Nothing
keeps these people down for ever, failure least of all.

The Mars-ruled person will look you straight in the
eye, with unabashed honesty and rather touching faith.
You're his friend, aren't you? You like him, don't you?
No? Then the tears will start, but inside. He'll never show
it on the surface, if he can help it. If you see him openly
weeping, you can be certain that he's been cut to the very
soul in some way. Aries would rather be caught dead than
be caught weak – and some of them literally risk the
former to avoid the latter.

The ram will seldom glance nervously around the room.
When he does, he's no longer interested in talking with
you. Something else has caught his attention, and for the
moment, you are forgotten. So is what you're saying.
Don't be offended. Remember the baby and his toes and
fingers.

He will undoubtedly be at the head of his chosen career
or involved in a profession on his own. If he's not, then
you can easily recognize him by the discontent he clearly
shows at being forced to submit to others. You can look
for a liberal attitude, lavish generosity with both time and
material things, and a marked desire to lead all the marches – with loud cymbals. But don't look for subtlety, tact
or humility. The average Arian was behind the barn door
when those qualities were passed out. He's a little short
on patience, too. In a coffee shop, he'll quickly criticize
the waitress and the sandwich, if the first is fresh and the
second is stale. But he'll probably leave an unnecessarily
big tip when the service is good.

Aries is very direct, to put it mildly. Deceptiveness
and deviousness are entirely foreign to the Mars nature.
Frankness and refreshing honesty are Arian trademarks,

yet rams don't make the best credit risks. Some of them lack stability and evidence a child-like lack of responsibility. Even those who have matured can forget debts in the excitement of the ever-present new challenge of the moment, which will always consume their entire attention. They'll eventually pay their bills cheerfully and willingly, but you may be out of breath when you catch up with them.

Although Aries is the firebrand, who forges his way through life with daring initiative and enterprise, there's a strange quirk to his bravery. He'll face the abominable snowman or the Frankenstein monster without the slightest trace of fear, yet he can't stand physical pain. He's never a moral coward, but he can be a huge sissy about anything that hurts. The dentist is not one of his favourite people.

Every Arian, at some time in his life, will indulge in rash behaviour that brings an injury to the head or face. Cuts and burns are also likely, and severe or even migraine headaches, which could stem from kidney infections. The ram would be wise to steel himself and see that dentist regularly, guard his eyesight, watch his diet, treat head colds seriously, and stay away from alcohol (not only bad for the kidneys, but quite combustible when combined with the Mars temper). Skin rashes, painful knee-caps and stomach disorders also plague those born in late March or April. The ram's constitution is strong and tough, if he doesn't abuse it, which he usually does, by ignoring it. When you see him confined to bed with little to say, you know he's really sick. Even so, it may require handcuffs to keep him down. He can survive fevers high enough to kill the average person, and many of them are brought on by his headstrong Mars tendency to carry

on under adverse circumstances, at the wrong times with
the wrong people. The angry impatience and frustration
this always triggers is the real cause of his health pro-
blems. His reaction to delay makes him ill, and the conscious cultivation of patience and cautious deliberation
would keep the doctor away. Not that he'll take such
advice. He keeps the doctor away for years at a time
anyhow, until he either drops in exhaustion or reaches an
age when he gets more sensible. There's not much danger
of an Aries becoming addicted to drugs. Normally, the
ram won't even take a sleeping pill. He'd much rather
stay wide awake. (He's afraid he might miss something.)

Because of his forceful optimism, Aries (along with the
other fire signs, Leo and Sagittarius) seldom falls victim
to the chronic, lingering diseases – which astrology has
always taught and medical science now realizes are triggered or intensified by melancholy and pessimism. The
fire signs are more susceptible to raging fevers, fulminat-
ing infections, strokes, high blood pressure and violently
acute illness. Say what you will about his impulsiveness,
the ram is seldom guilty of gloom. The seeds of depression,
even if planted, will die a quick death in Arian soil. But
that precious idea Aries holds, that no one else can do
anything as efficiently as he can, may run away with him
and lead to a thousand disasters. He'll carry through his
schemes with dash and confidence, seldom realizing that
he's overreaching himself and headed for ulcers or a nervous breakdown. No one ever accuses him of laziness.

Because of their guileness nature, subtle tricks of strategy are impossible for these people. One Aries I know
well, with his fiery, contagious enthusiasm, got a financial
angel to back one of his original ideas. Just as the deal
was about to be closed, and this ram was about to realize

his fondest dreams, the angel logically suggested that a well-known expert oversee the operation. The Aries was positive that no one could run it as well as himself, and he was fearful of getting involved with someone from whom he might have to take orders, so he responded quickly, with the usual Aries humility. He waved his cigar in the air in a superior gesture, and asked bluntly, 'How do you want your no, fast or slow?' The financial angel just as quickly withdrew his backing, and the poor Aries promoter soon developed a severe case of business leprosy. For many frustrating months, those who had formerly been behind him one hundred per cent were mysteriously out to lunch or in Europe every time he called.

A little tactful diplomacy could have kept his dream from exploding, but it takes the average ram many years to reach the diplomacy of an Arian like Dean Rusk. People who have arrived at the top through hard and patient work justifiably resent an aggressive Aries, who thinks he knows far more with far less experience. He learns modesty and humility only after many dismal failures. But once he's learned, he can make a project pay off like a gusher, adding stacks of creative ideas, and intuitively making the right moves. He reaches leadership only by first respecting those above him in credit and stature, yet success, when it comes, is normally gigantic and impressive. Strangely, most Aries people often create wealth for others rather than for themselves. Lots of rams pay rent most of their lives, and seldom own their own home. It doesn't seem to break the Mars spirit that cash doesn't always cling to him, perhaps because what he seeks is not necessarily in the bank.

Though Aries pushes ahead with confidence, caring little for the feelings of others, and his attitude, especially in youth, is 'me first', he can be the warmest and most generous of all the Sun signs. He's not cruel. He just honestly believes that he can do anything better than anyone else, and he's psychologically unable to stand by while others fumble and flop. Give him a choice of money or glory, and he'll take glory any time. He's as fond of a dollar as the next person, but he's just a few shades fonder of praise and fame. The ram has a way of making instant decisions without the authority of his superiors. His speech can be satirical and cutting in invective. Arian anger flashes forth with the speed of sound, but it's usually gone before the victim knows what it's all about, and the happy, child-like smile quickly returns. One can't help being reminded of a certain impulsive ram, Nikita Khrushchev, who once banged his shoe in a fit of childish temper, on a table at the United Nations, in full view of a television audience, and the devil-take-the-hindmost. He was being ignored, and what Arian cares about tact when he's being ignored? Yet this same Aries was truly heartbroken when he missed enjoying the magic wonder of Disneyland.

Mars people are often accused of having a terrible temper. They have. But they also have a complete inability to remain angry, and once over with, the grievance is generally buried and forgotten. He's hurt and surprised that you still remember the rash things he said but didn't mean. Given the chance, Aries will apologize to his worst enemy, regardless of any dire threats he made in the throes of emotion. He seeks acceptance, even while he heedlessly and deliberately courts rejection. Aries people seldom become angry with individuals. You may get the shower of sparks, but the fire is actually directed towards an idea or a situation he finds intolerable.

The ram is capable of trying to tell a small white lie, if it will put him foremost or save one of his cherished ideals, but most of the time, he has little use for lies, which is fortunate, because he gets caught every time. Blunt candour is quicker, and since the main interest is in getting to the point in a hurry, he prefers to tell the truth. He has no time at all for gossip. That involves discussing others, and Aries is far too interested in himself to waste any excess energy speculating on the inner secrets, behaviour or motives of anyone else. Besides, people are normally either black or white to him. He doesn't bother with the grey tones. Don't mistake this for prejudice, however. If he has heavy planetary afflictions on his natal chart, the Aries impulsive disregard for the facts may come forth in the form of cruelty or prejudice; but this is extremely rare. The typical ram will dine with beggars and kings with equal ease and genuine affection. Any reputation he gets for prejudice comes from his tendency to lump people into two distinct camps – his friends and his enemies – and he'll expect you to line them up the same way, if you're close to him.

Despite his shocking forwardness, the ram can also be the epitome of social grace. He can converse for hours in an exciting, interesting manner on subjects he knows absolutely nothing about. There's a lot of surface polish to cover that aggressive Mars drive. Patience with detail isn't his strong point. He'd rather leave the minor, petty statistics to someone else. That's sensible enough. Someone else would handle them far more efficiently. Time spent pinning down the facts is resented, because the ram cares nothing for yesterday's lessons, and tomorrow is too far away to worry about. Today is his natural residence.

This hour and this minute. He's totally consumed in the action of the present.

A realist, yet a decided idealist, Aries often defies emotional description. No one can show such tough, forceful behaviour. Yet, few others are capable of such sentimentality, wistful innocence and belief in miracles. Mars people are literally incapable of accepting defeat. They won't recognize it – even when it stares them in the face. They're incurable optimists about the end result of anything from love to a baseball game. Being very clever in-fighters, the rams battle best with their heads, meaning their minds. They enjoy opposition because of the challenge it presents, and they'll go out of their way to meet an obstacle and conquer it long before it comes to them – and often when it might have been headed in the opposite direction. They don't wait around for success to drop in their laps, either. They'll chase it at a furious pace, which is why you'll find very few Arians on welfare lists.

Just thinking about the energy of the ram wears out most people. But Arians are also capable of being calm, wise and serious when they choose. Unfortunately, they usually don't choose until youth has passed and maturity has mellowed their rash idealism and sense of driving haste. They can arouse popular sympathy easily, yet they don't necessarily make good politicians. Thomas Jefferson and Eugene McCarthy are rare exceptions to the rule. Of all the Arians who have tossed their hats in the ring, most have had comparatively brief or troubled political careers. There hasn't been an Aries president in the United States since John Tyler in 1840. The field of politics is difficult for the average ram. For one thing, he's not the very best economist in the world. For another, he's impulsive in his speech and he hates to hedge, both deadly traits for a politician. Most politicians wait to see what people want before airing their positions. The average Aries has his own ideas of what the people need, never mind what they want, and he'll see that they get it, sooner than might be politically expedient. Still, he's so idealistic, that once the Arian has come before the public, he fires their imagination and makes them believe in themselves again. The freshness of Mars candour can blow through the smoke of political back rooms like a breeze.

But most Aries people are usually happier in business or the creative arts, where they're so desperately needed. Others may excel in planning strategy. Calmer heads and more practical minds may be better at efficient organization. But without the direct action, energy and originality of the rams, the most desirable projects would fall to the ground or make little headway.

You may find an occasional Arian who is shy, but you'll never find one who's uncertain where he stands. It's difficult to express your own individuality around these people. Aries is far happier when he's talking about himself and his plans than about anybody or anything else (with the exception of the loved one, when he's caught in the clutches of a romance). Once you get his interest – and lots of luck – he'll be an attentive listener, especially if your ideas are exciting and progressive. He'll promote you to the skies, and offer you his time, money, sympathy and loyalty. When you're in the hospital, he may forget to send a card, but he may choose the hospital for you, drive you there himself and refer you to his own doctor (who will be superior to Pasteur and both of the Mayo brothers, of course). Once involved in helping you through a rough time, Aries will walk the extra mile without hesitation. But show your gratitude, please. He'll be deeply hurt, if not downright angry, when you don't appreciate his strenuous actions, which went far beyond the call of duty, and also probably far beyond what you needed or wanted. He enjoys doing favours; the larger the charitable gesture the better; but the ram wants his credit when it's coming to him. If thanks are withheld, however, it probably won't keep him from helping again. His amazing faith in himself is matched only by his naïve trust in others, which is why he's almost constantly disillusioned, and complaining that someone has let him down. Of course, he won't stay down long. He'll pick himself up, dust himself off, and soon be ready, willing and able to blast away again, after a typical binge of violent but brief depression.

The ram gives such an impression of sincerity that it's startling to face his sheer audacity when he claims for a fact something he knows – or should know – to be untrue. Accuse him of dishonesty, and he'll look at you in amazement, with candid eyes open wide in utter horror that you could doubt him. He can wear blinkers and ear plugs to shut out anything he doesn't want to believe. Even when his position is completely untenable, he'll bravely stick to his guns and work for the lost cause with earnest conviction. Still, he can change his mind about an opinion you thought he was born with in a moment of fast decision, and when he does, it's impossible for him to regain his former point of view, let alone remember it. His urge to toss the past in the trash can and go forward at full speed (one of the chief reasons he adapts to new locations and people so painlessly), makes him think those who try to reason with him are interfering with his progress. Then he's liable to throw what little tact he has to the four winds. The ultra-conservative, who weighs every word and decision, is maddening to the Mars souls, who can communicate their annoyance and frustration with clear and abundant meaning. So it's easy to see why they sometimes make such bitter enemies of older, wiser heads.

Aries has an innocent wistful facet to his nature, and a kind of eternal, joyous naïve faith, blended with the blind zeal of the born crusader. Like the diamond, his Mars horns are hard, and tough to crack.

He sees bright red frequently, but when the sparks have disappeared, he becomes as cheerful and openly friendly as the happy Arian daisy. His metal is iron, and its unbendable strength gives him nine times as many lives to live as others; nine times as many chances of winning the battle. The fire that consumes his spirit can be a flaming torch that lights the way to courage for anyone who recognizes his great idealism.

He is the pioneer, always leading others onward to an impossible goal. His beautiful iron faith is pure – unmixed with the alloys of hypocrisy and greed. He seldom amasses a fortune, and if he did, he would be too busy to stop and count it. Help yourself to his money, clothes or time. He always has some to spare, however pressed or poor he may be temporarily. The ram knows that bread cast on the waters not only feeds his ego and returns again increased, but it makes people happy, one of the things he enjoys most in life. To Aries, miracles are a dime a dozen. If you run out, he'll make you some more, wrapped in brave, scarlet dreams.

Famous Aries Personalities

Dean Acheson	Charles Chaplin	Henry James
Bismarck	Julie Christie	Thomas Jefferson
Marlon Brando	Joan Crawford	Nikita Khrushchev
Clare Boothe Luce	Leopold Stokowski	Harry Houdini
Henry Luce	Gloria Swanson	Peter Ustinov
Eugene McCarthy	Arturo Toscanini	Vincent Van Gogh
Joseph Pulitzer	Bette Davis	Andrew Lloyd Webber
Simone Signoret	Thomas Dewey	Tennessee Williams

The Aries Man

He said, 'I go my ways
And when I find a mountain-rill
I set it in a blaze . . .

'So either way
I'll get into the garden,
and I don't care what happens.'

That creature over there making a phone call – is it an electrically charged dynamo? Is it a flaming torch? Is it a bird, an explosion – or is it Superman? Well, practically. It's an Aries male, which is pretty close. Let's hope you know what you're looking for. Should it be excitement, an Aries man will provide it by the bushel, with seldom a dull moment to blur the sparkle. But if you're looking for the security and contentment of a soothing love, you're in the wrong telephone booth.

Aries can overwhelm you with passionate ardour one minute, and be as icy as a polar bear the next. Insult him or lose his interest – either or both – and that warm, impulsive Mars nature will freeze instantly. To ignite it again may mean starting all over from Act One, Scene One.

Aries men are fairly bursting with ideas and creative energy. Keeping up with him may be tiring, but keep up you'd better. At least mentally. Aries has a way of leaving the snails behind and not glancing back. He'll probably look and act younger than springtime, which is all very delightful, but his youthful aura may carry over into his mental and emotional attitudes until he's matured, which won't be early in life. The Aries man is impatient with slow pokes, bold and confident, always ahead of others, and sometimes ahead of himself as well. He can be the soul of generosity, giving his time, money, sympathy and possessions by the carload cheerfully to strangers. But he can also be exasperatingly intolerant, thoughtless, selfish and demanding, when his desires are delayed, or he's forced to be around negative people.

When it comes to love, his heedless attitude is absolutely amazing. He'll plunge into an affair, positive that this is the only true love ever known by any two people ever born, with the possible exception of Romeo and Juliet. When it breaks in half, he'll pick up the pieces, and try every angle he can think of to salvage the dead romance. If it's beyond repair, he'll start all over again with a new Juliet, and it will be like the very first time. No matter how many romantic mistakes he makes, the ram is sure his true love or soul mate is just around the next dream. Unless you're a Scorpio female, the Aries man is as passionate as any woman could ask. There's little left to desire. He's so idealistic and susceptible to sentiment, he'll squeeze all the tingles, sighs, ecstasies and poetry it's possible to squeeze out of a relationship. Aries isn't capable of going halfway. He gives all of himself to the burning interest of the moment.

You may be involved with one of the quieter sheep. Don't let him fool you. He's still ruled by Mars. He doesn't talk much right away? He's not openly exuberant and pushy? Yes, I know one, too. But take my word for it, if you could see inside that hard head, you would discover that his brain is spinning at approximately two hundred revolutions per second. Any time you meet this kind, one who doesn't at first appear to have the typical Mars drive, check the present record of the business he's conducting. You'll soon be convinced you're dealing with an Aries. Then ask his ex-girlfriends. They'll probably answer with a giggle. 'Him? Bashful? Timid? You must mean someone else.' After a while, you should begin to get the picture. That quiet demeanour is a mask for a fiery heart and a tough business drive. Naturally, it's easier when you're in love with a plain, simple ram, who makes it obvious just how enthusiastic he is about everything from potato chips to moonlight and motor trips.

No other Sun sign can be so scrupulously faithful as Aries when he's really in love for keeps. His honesty will usually keep him from fooling you, and his idealism will keep him from wanting to. Promiscuity or even light flirtations are not an Arian habit, no matter what the books tell you. Not when he's deeply involved with all his heart. He's looking for a storybook romance, and storybook romances never include a casual attitude towards love and sex. Those other girls were BYCA (before you came along). In fact, I know one Aries who frequently precedes discussions of yesterday with his current flame with, 'That was BU' (before us).

Of course, you must keep alert to future possibilities, because as sincere as he is in his present devotion and promises of complete loyalty (which are undoubtedly absolutely true), his need for romance is so strong that he's capable of looking elsewhere if you don't keep his illusions alive constantly. The minute you let your mutual love lose its storybook flavour, he may wander off the steady path. In case you're not sure, storybook love, to him, does not include going to dreamland at night with a female who has Vicks salve on her chest to clear up her

cough. It also does not include watching your intimate
personal toilette, such as polishing your nails, whitening
your teeth, brightening your hair with 'blondes have more
fun' bleach, peeling your sunburn, filing your nails or
fighting with your mother for hours on the phone. Somehow, in his mind, this is not the way storybook princesses
behave. And goodness knows, Juliet would never have sat
with her feet up, chewing gum and watching TV. Wear
your perfume when he's around, and giggle with your girl
friends when he's not. He finds it difficult to visualize
himself as Prince Charming when he kisses you awake
and you either snore, or shout unpleasantly, 'For gosh
sakes, let me sleep, will you?' Now, really, is that the way
Sleeping Beauty would have acted when she woke up? Be
prepared to greet him dewy-eyed and breathless each
morning, fresh from your dreams, thrilled to find his hand-
some face so near. And let him know it.

Aries males whose sweethearts neglect romance are
heartbroken at first. Then they become angry. Then they
go looking for a princess who doesn't snore and things
like that. This isn't dishonest as far as he's concerned. He
didn't break a promise. You did. You made him think
you were a lovely nightingale, singing in the moonlight,
like it says in his favourite song. Now he finds out you're
a chattering squirrel or a nagging blue jay and the jolt
rouses him from his heavenly world of angelic choirs and
bells ringing every time he touches your hand. How can
bells ring when your hands are always full of dirty ashtrays,
and how can he hear choirs when you're screaming at
him that he stayed out until after midnight for two nights
in a row? (Which he did, of course, but who are you to
think you can dictate his every move? Marriage is not a
prison, and you are not his warden – that's his attitude.)

If you learn how to open your eyes and look at him mistily and all the rest of it, he'll stay with you happily, and ignore every female on earth for you. The ram is highly unlikely to commit himself physically to more than one woman at a time (unless there's a Gemini ascendant or some Venus affliction in his natal chart). It just wouldn't fit his image of one true and lasting love. The decision to break off the old will always be made before becoming too deeply involved with the new. You'll have plenty of warning. An Aries man can rarely pretend a passion he doesn't feel. This alone prevents any undue amount of deception. Besides, now you know how to keep him inside the pages of that storybook.

Just don't be dull, negative or overly timid. To hold him, you'll have to be a combination of Grace Kelly, Ursula Andress, Marie Dressler, Madame Curie and Queen Victoria, with a little bit of Clare Boothe Luce thrown in. No one princess will ever satisfy his image of the ideal. It's quite a trick to convince him you're superior to all other females, but it will keep him spotlessly faithful, if you can swing it. It's really worth a try, because, if the Aries plunge into romance is headlong, his race out of it is equally reckless. He's both an idealist and an egotist, which means he hates to admit he's wrong, or that the love he chose could die. Still, always remember that he's capable of finding situations unbearable that others would consider par for the course. After a separation, if you catch him in the right mood, you can fire his romance all over again, if you act as if there had never been any previous intimacy. You'll have to play hard to get, because he loves a challenge. To make it easier to forgive him, if trouble ever arises, remember that any straying was due to a sudden impulse after his nightingale stopped singing

in the moonlight, not to a deliberate seeking of casual
variety. Adultery is actually distasteful to his honest
nature. Don't fret about the future. You have the magic
key to his heart. Lock it.

If you have any ideas about playing games with him
by flirting – drop them. Your first indiscretion will probably be your last. You can lose him with just a whisper
or an intimate look at another man, let alone any actual
infidelity. He insists on being first in everything, and you
can bet your old pressed gardenia this includes being first
in your heart. Aries is possessive and jealous in the
extreme. Only a Leo male can get wilder at the thought
of a transgression on the part of his beloved. To make it
worse, the ram will never give you the blind faith he
expects you to give him in such matters. You'll simply
have to understand that his animated conversations with
other women are innocent, because he'll demand all the
freedom of social contact he denies to you, and then more.
Your Mars lover will glue you to a pedestal, and expect
you to stay there. Don't move a single toe. Don't even
look as if you want to.

The Aries is a natural rebel. He loves to defy authority
and he thinks he was born smarter than anyone else.
Perhaps he was, but most people don't relish being told
so. Thanks to his rash way of pushing his superiority, he's
liable to fall flat on his face more than once. Because of
his need to lead and refusal to follow, those in more
powerful positions will teach him frequent lessons in
humility. At these times, you're way ahead, because he'll
run to you for comfort and assurance when his ego is
bruised. Then you'll learn that, beneath his self-confident,
aggressive front, lies an inferiority complex he'd rather die
than admit having. The woman who handles his shattered

confidence with gentle and total devotion has the best chance of keeping his heart permanently. Never make the mistake of agreeing with his momentary enemy, or trying to be fair and seeing the other side of the controversy. You must love what he loves and hate what he hates. He demands the same fierce and unquestioning loyalty that he gives, in both love and friendship. It's his code. Unless you honour it, find another man.

There are no subtle tricks in the Aries nature. It's not at all hard to recognize when a Mars man is finished with a relationship. The ice and boredom in his voice and manner will be unmistakable, and will usually be accompanied by a frank statement that makes it crystal clear. On the other hand, an explosive flame of scorching anger is less serious, signifying that his displeasure is probably just a passing mood, and the romance can be saved. You have more reason to fear his ice than his fire.

Aries males don't like games. He'll be direct in all his approaches. And that means in romance, as well as in business. He won't waste a second, once the love has been recognized, but be sure to let him be the one to recognize it. Don't chase him, phone him frequently, get starry-eyed or declare your feelings until you're absolutely sure the passion is mutual. The quickest way to lose him is to make the first advance. He must be the leader here, as elsewhere. If you don't allow him to be, he can lose interest so fast it can astonish you and crush you at the same time. Once you're each firmly committed, however, don't be too cool and casual, or he'll seek attention somewhere else. Love with an Aries man is like walking a tightrope between warm interest and aloof detachment. You practically have to be a trapeze artist. Don't run after him. Don't run away from him, either. Stick a penny in your shoe, carry a four-leaf clover and wish on a star. That will get you as far as any normal, methodical strategy. Maybe further. You have to keep him guessing, even after you're his. At the same time, he needs the assurance that your love is always there. Learn to live with it – or learn to live without an Aries.

On the plus side, although your Aries lover will insist on being first in the relationship, he'll also be the first to say he's sorry after a quarrel, and the first to be there when you need him. He'll be right by your side when you're ill or unhappy. He'll spend money on you freely and willingly (if he's a typical son of Mars). He'll compliment your appearance, appreciate your talents and be a stimulating mental companion. Although he can be bossy and lose his temper over a trifle, he'll seldom let the sun go down on his anger before making up. You may be the most important thing in his life, but he'll expect you to know that, and wait for affection and attention when he's all excited by some new idea which is consuming his interest. He wants to be your whole world, but unlike other men, he'll let you share his world, if you're his equal.

The Aries male will expect his lady fair to be ultra-feminine and a tomboy at the same time. He wants you to be completely independent, yet willing to stay a few paces behind him. He'll expect you to praise him and be devoted to him, but never play the role of humble slavey. Are you still with me? Good. Brave girl. There's more to come. He's capable of saying bitterly cruel and sarcastic things to you when his ego has been wounded, things he won't mean at all, but which may break your heart if you don't understand him. Then he'll expect you to forgive and forget as readily as he does. You'll have to like all his friends, while he reserves the right to be bored by yours. Well, you wanted a man, didn't you? You've sure got one in your Aries mate. If you're a real woman, your love affair can be the envy of everyone in town, just like Romeo and Juliet (without the tragedy, of course).

Once you've married him, the Aries male will dominate the home or leave it. He won't stand for being nagged in public or private, especially about how he spends his dough. He earned it, didn't he? It's *his* money, isn't it? (Sometimes that possessive pronoun can stretch to include the money you earn, too.) He may not balance the budget too well – and I'm being kind to put it so tactfully – but don't take it over yourself, even if you made straight As in maths. Never question his financial affairs. It's essential that he control the purse-strings all the way. He'll be generous with his cash, if he's a typical Arian, and give you whatever you need. You can have that cobra skin handbag after he's bought that alligator briefcase, if there's anything left over. (He may be a little selfish, but he's never stingy.)

Though the ram may change jobs frequently until he becomes his own boss, he won't let you starve. He'll find a way to keep the dollars flowing in, even though they may flow out again just as fast. Better save a few pence in the blue china pig and surprise him with it when he needs it most, because he's not likely to salt away much of his earnings himself (unless he has a hidden asset, like the Moon in Capricorn or Cancer, or an ascendant which dictates economy).

Each new baby will find him behaving like the devoted proud papa of your dreams. Later, he may be a little bossy with the children, and try to dictate their careers. He'll be a warm and wonderful fun daddy, but he might have to be reminded that the youngsters need independence as much as he does. Fatherhood is definitely a role he'll enjoy. Baseball, talks about the birds and bees, football, father–daughter dinners, the whole works. Just don't let him think little Herman or Henrietta is more important to you than he is, however, or his enjoyment of the role may cool considerably.

Go ahead and continue your career after marriage if you like. He probably won't resent it, as long as you don't outshine him. It's easier to forgive instant suppers or quick-frozen kumquats than to forgive your lack of faith in his ideas. That's important to remember.

Encourage his independence, but try to curb his impulsiveness – tactfully. He must lead or life is worth little to him. His great and bubbly enthusiasm can die a sad death if you douse it with wet blankets or short-circuit his positive energy with negative thinking. The minute he loses authority on the job or in the home, his refreshing optimism will turn to moody discontent and finally, complete disinterest. It's not his nature to submit. He's a man's man. Never destroy his masculinity, but never lose your own individuality. Don't try to push him around, and don't let him push you around. An Aries husband won't put up with a wife who runs around to club meetings every night. Neither will he tolerate a wife who sits home and crochets bedspreads and tablecloths all day. You'll have to aim somewhere in the middle. If you're successful, just think – you'll be the only white-haired Juliet in your crowd someday, with a husband who's still sentimental on your golden wedding anniversary. That's quite a challenge if you're a romantic, and of course you are, or you wouldn't be involved with an Aries man in the first place.

The Aries Woman

'But aren't you going to run and help her?'
Alice asked . . .
'No use, no use!' said the King.
'She runs so fearfully quick
you might as well try to catch a Bandersnatch!'

So you're in love with an Aries girl. I don't know whether to congratulate you or sympathize with you.

When Byron wrote that 'Man's love is of man's life a thing apart; 'tis woman's whole existence', he forgot about the Aries woman. She may think love is her whole existence, but she's too vitally absorbed in the world around her, not to mention in herself, for it to be the beginning and end of her life. She can get along without a man easier than any female you'll ever meet.

Of course, getting along without a man is not the same thing as getting along without romance. She'll always need that hero of her dreams to yearn for in her heart. He may be long ago and faraway – or hiding just out of sight and touch, somewhere in tomorrow's mists – but she'll think about him in an April rain. He'll haunt her when the first snow falls, when she hears a certain song or sees lightning flash. However, while she's yearning, if there's no male around in actual physical presence, she won't miss him terribly. Anything he could do, she can do better – she thinks.

The Aries girl will open her own doors. She'll also put on her own coat, fight her own battles, pull out her own chair, hail her taxi and light her cigarette without any masculine help. Doing it herself is, to her, the fastest way to get it done. Naturally, this doesn't set too well on the vulnerable male ego. The Mars girl is determined to take the lead, to be the first to move to action, and that includes the action of making the first advance in romance. Aries females are the most likely of all the Sun signs to do the proposing, especially if the man is slow about naming the date. And that's about as early as you can safely show your feelings – when she proposes. Before that you're taking a chance. Be very careful about moving in on an Aries girl. She wants to be the leader in the love affair. Better be sure you have her heart safely in your pocket before you try to grab her around the waist and kiss her goodnight. Otherwise, she may give you a sharp right hook to the jaw and run like a frightened deer.

Don't be misled. The reason for her running isn't maidenly modesty. She's not afraid of your passionate intentions. Those she can handle. Her flight is based on the fear of getting tangled up with a worshipping slave or a lovestruck puppy dog, either one of whom would bore her to tears. Be casual, keep her guessing, and the chances are she'll chase you into a corner instead. A man who resists her impact always intrigues an Aries female. She can't understand why she isn't overwhelming him with her obvious charms. Then her Mars ego will leave no stone unturned to prove she's desirable, even when she has no lasting interest in him.

Scarlett O'Hara is the very epitome of the Mars-ruled Aries female. Like Scarlett, the Aries girl will gather every available male for a hundred miles around to her feet, while her wilful heart yearns for the one man she can't have for one reason or another. Like Scarlett, the Mars woman can quickly adapt for survival if necessary, without whimpering. Both the O'Hara and the Aries characters are tough enough to defy convention, face an advancing army, or even shoot a man through the head with icy calmness, if he threatens her loved ones.

Never was Scarlett more Mars-like than when she was starving, alone and friendless, and without waiting for a man to come to the rescue, she clenched her fist towards heaven and shouted, 'I'll survive this . . . and when I do, I'll never be hungry again . . . If I have to lie, cheat, steal or kill – as God is my witness, I'll never be hungry again!' Much later, her emotions shattered, her beloved child dead and the one man she loved about to walk out of her life, this typical Aries woman was still able to say, 'I'll think of some way to get him back. There's never been a man I couldn't get, once I set my mind on him . . . After all, tomorrow is another day.'

Yes, Scarlett O'Hara creates a vivid image of the first Sun sign of the zodiac, with all the Mars strength and ability to bounce back after tragedy; able to play the female role to the hilt, with fluttering lashes and a well-timed tear, but just as able to take over a man's job when the men aren't around. A careful study of Scarlett's character can give you an excellent understanding of what you're in for with an Aries woman – and naturally, also the rewards you can look forward to after you've been brave enough to claim her. Her aggressive drive may be hard to take, but her shining optimism and faith in tomorrow can be mighty uplifting.

The Aries girl is rather a pushover for flattery, if it has an honest base. Let her know you admire her, but don't be too flowery or sugary about it. Her loyalty in love is gigantic, as long as you keep the sentiment alive, for she is deeply sentimental. There's the typical Arian contradic-

tion in her: she doesn't want to be obviously chased, yet
she quickly loses interest if you're too detached. She
doesn't want a completely domineering male, but neither
will she warm up to a man who sits adoringly at her feet.
Before love can bring her happiness, the Aries woman
must meet the eternal Mars challenge – her strong desire
to control the lover, conflicting with her secret wish to be
controlled *by him*. Unbelievably idealistic, sometimes she
searches in vain for that brave knight in shining armour,
who will sweep her off her feet, conquer the world, hand
it to her gently and yet never sacrifice his manhood. Since
he exists only in fairy tales and the myths of King Arthur's
court, the Aries woman often walks alone, without a star
to guide her. Her days are bright and full of excitement,
her nights are sometimes dark and full of longing. Yet,
when her defeated dreams become smouldering ashes –
just as you think the flame is dying, Aries leaps up to
build another fire.

She must be proud of you to love you. But don't be so
important that you neglect to notice *her* talents and abilities. Though she'll demand a lot from you, she'll give
double measure in return. The Aries girl can be generous
to a fault with her time and sympathy, cheerfully sharing
her possessions and money, but when it comes to love,
she's downright stingy. 'What's hers is hers' in the
romance department, and it will take very little to set off
a jealous explosion. Don't admire your favourite movie
actress in her hearing, or pay too many compliments to
her girl friends. The man with an Aries wife is safer with
a male secretary. If she's not first with you in every way,
you'll soon wonder where all the intense passion and
thrilling emotion went so fast. When the Aries woman
has been really hurt, she turns from fire to ice. Her fire

burns hot and dies quickly. Her ice can be eternal. Memorize that, if you care deeply about her – and it's doubtful that she'll stand for your caring about her any other way. Aries plays for keeps.

She puts the loved one on a pedestal, expecting him to live up to an impossible image of perfection, stubbornly refusing to look at his clay feet, until they become too muddy for even her to miss. Never criticize the lover, husband or children of an Aries woman unless you're wearing an asbestos suit. She's capable of being demanding, selfish, and making cutting remarks when you dampen her hopeful plans. Yet, she can also be gentle, devoted and co-operative when she's met halfway.

Since she prefers the company of men to women, and solicits admiration from every male she meets, be he nine or ninety, you'll have plenty of chances to feel the stabs of those little green monsters of jealousy. Forget it. As fiercely possessive as she is of you, she won't put up with your possessiveness of her for an instant. The Aries girl insists on complete freedom, before and after marriage. You'll have to trust her wherever she goes and whatever she does, though she won't have that kind of faith in you (unless she's learned the hard way to keep her emotions under control if it kills her, which it almost will). It's not as bad as it sounds, because she'll be faithful, once she's really yours. An Aries girl is seldom able to love two men at the same time. She's simply too honest for such deception. Barring unusual circumstances, she'll let you know clearly that love is dead before going ahead in total commitment to someone else.

This woman is capable of deep passion and mystical idealism, woven together in strange patterns. In any relationship she feels is real and for ever after, there will be no holding back, no feminine wiles; coquettish tricks or silly games. Her love, like her speech and actions, is direct. There's something clean and fresh about the utter simplicity of her emotions, but even so, they often get her into waters way over her head. You may have to tame her a little, but she'll accept it with surprising docility if she really loves you.

Mars females are often career girls. They can handle almost any profession a man can handle, from stockbroking to real estate. They can also turn a nice ankle or profile in strictly feminine occupations like modelling and acting. It may be difficult to get her to give up her job for you, if it's a real career or profession. She may toss it overboard for a period, while she's suffused with the glow of romance and picturing a storybook cottage for two beside the sea (typical of the Arian imagination that leads straight to the happy part and ignores the dull part). But when the cottage begins to need a paint job, the roof starts to leak and the first fine rapture dims slightly, she may be anxious to dig out her social security card again. She'll be far happier and more loving – even more gentle – if she's allowed to fill her idle hours with something that interests her. Mars emotions, unfulfilled, can look for molehills of frustrations to build into huge mountains of trouble.

There's practically nothing this woman won't tackle. If it's a challenge or just something she thinks she wants to brighten her life, she'll make some kind of a stab at it whether it's practical or not. I know an Aries woman who was forced for financial reasons to live for several years in two rooms with a husband, five active children and a dog. That kind of an arrangement can get a little cramped, and just contemplating it might give a woman with any

THE ARIES WOMAN 33

common sense a few doubts. Not a Mars female. This one coped somehow, though she may have let it goad her into a few tantrums. In the middle of the situation, when an astrologer read her natal chart, and pointed out that her planetary aspects showed a long period of great hardships in her life, she was puzzled and intrigued. 'When does it look like it might happen?' she wanted to know.

This same impulsive Aries woman got a sudden urge one day to add another dog to the group camping out in two rooms. She felt the family's male pet needed a female companion. He looked lonesome. Besides, the children thought it was a rollicking good idea. The discovery that the second dog wasn't house-broken threw her only temporarily. Like a determined drill sergeant, she assigned every member of the family their turn at scrubbing the carpet. After she saw that it would never be the same again, she surveyed the situation and made a decision. To get rid of the second dog? Of course not. She was secretly hoping there would be puppies some day soon. The money would just have to come from somewhere to get a new rug. Funny thing – it did. As for the puppies, she was sure some miracle would happen to move the entire crowd into a new apartment before the happy event. Funny thing – it did. Miracles have a way of happening to those who believe in them. Aries women certainly believe. Sometimes to the point of foolishness. Her rash ways can get her into some complicated pickles, and she may have a few grey hairs before she learns how to avoid the same pickle twice. Aries is not noted for learning from experience. The spirit is willing, but the disposition is headstrong. There's no use to try to caution a typical Aries female with the biblical warning, 'Pride goeth before a fall'. Her interpretation of the phrase, since she first heard it in Sunday School, is 'When your pride goes, you fall'.

Never worry that your Aries girl will succumb to the charms of a wolf. She's immune to wolves and playboys, and in far more danger of being seduced by an idealist with a cause, preferably a lost cause. But even with him, she'll assert her individuality frequently. It will never be completely conquered in the Mars woman, though it can be subdued by the right man. She'll buy you gifts, loan you money, nurse you through illness, and help you get a job. And she'll expect the same from you.

She'll deny it vehemently (she does almost everything vehemently), but when she's miserable, you should be miserable. When she's happy, you should he happy. To Aries, love is equal sharing. She'll expect to share your razor, your bank account, your friendships and your dreams. In return, you can share hers. Of course, her razor may be broken, her bank account a little overdrawn, her friendships slightly scattered and her dreams too large for you to swallow. But she's not selfish with them. Keeping a secret from her can drive her wild, and it's not a good idea to drive an Aries wild. Don't ever embarrass her by your grammar, clothing or behaviour in public. She won't embarrass you, at least not in these matters.

To injure her pride or dampen her enthusiasm will almost break her heart. Others will constantly be doing just that to her. The world resents a female who talks back to it, and who thinks she's smarter than everyone else. When she discovers she really doesn't run the universe after all, she'll come running into your arms in tears, her world all dark and dismal. Then you'll have a chance to see her as she really is, defenceless and vulnerable in the extreme, for all her outer confidence. She's not really

Tugboat Annie. She'd just like to be. She admires strength and tries to imitate it. The Aries idealism and optimistic faith in human nature is often dashed to bits by reality. Comfort her with tenderness at these times, and you'll probably never lose her. Always defend her against her enemies. She can never forgive you if you fail to fight for her or take her side. (But be prepared to make up with them when she does, which may be quickly.) At least she's fair about it. She'll also defend you. An Aries woman will throw away fame or fortune defiantly right in the face of anyone who hurts a friend of hers. If she loves you, her indignation will have no bounds. These women are nothing if not loyal.

As a wife, she may be quite a handful. There will probably be outside interests, because home will seldom be enough for her creative energies. Don't expect her to be a happy little cricket, chirping away contentedly by the hearth. She'll be a competent enough cook, and she'll keep the house spanking clean – at least, the part that shows. She'll sew on buttons and iron shirts, too, but she won't like it. Still, she'll do it when it's necessary. (An Aries woman can do almost anything when it's necessary.) Her fire is more like that of a glittering diamond than like the warm, comforting glow of the fireplace. There's undeniably a brittle side to her nature, and she may agitate you more often than she soothes you. But she's exciting and certainly never boring. Then there are always those moments of softness that belie her strong drive – for a man who has the patience to bring them out. Mars women are always softer inside than any but those who have been really close to them ever know. Her conversation will be very intelligent and very frequent. Don't hide behind the newspaper at breakfast. She'll expect companionship from you, or you can just scramble your own eggs.

You'll rarely find her complaining of illness or fatigue. But when she's in pain, she'll expect tons of sympathy. Although you may have to sit on her to get her to go to bed when she has a raging fever, be prepared to wait on her hand and foot when she has a toothache.

This is not the woman to call and tell you'll be working late at the office, unless you enjoy creating Fifth of November fireworks in the middle of February. She won't mind keeping the gravy hot, but she won't like not knowing where you really are, and what you're really doing, and she may call back to find out. The Aries wife will probably make an excellent impression on your boss, if you can keep her from telling him how to run his business. She won't mind going out to bring home the bacon when you're temporarily out of a job, but she can never respect a man who makes less money than she does (though an Aries woman would never leave a man for this reason – she'd be more inclined to make excuses for him). If she has a rare spell of letting herself go, the first word of disapproval from you will send her flying back to the mirror and perfume bottle. (In this way, she's as feminine as Eve herself.) A flattering comment about your secretary's new hair style will do the same thing, but it's more dangerous. Besides, you were warned to hire a male secretary. There's a vain streak in a Mars woman which makes her sensitive about everything from her age to an innocent remark about how tired she looks, which she may take as a hint that you think she looks like an old hag.

Keep the passion and romance alive in your marriage, or she'll be miserably unhappy. Aries will waste little time changing any situation which causes unhappiness, and that can lead to a hasty separation or an impulsive divorce. In most cases, letting her handle the family chequebook would be unwise, but you can try it, if the bank is game.

As a mother, she'll see that the baby is clean, happy, healthy and loved. She probably won't pick him up every time he cries, fuss over him or over-protect him. But her children will get lots of warm, impulsive kisses and bear hugs. An April mother will teach her youngsters to believe in leprechauns. She'll take them for walks in the park, and point out the sparkling necklaces left on the lawn by the fairies when they danced under the moon where others might see only the early morning dew on the grass. Aries women create a magic world of fantasy for their children. It's where they live themselves. She won't be a permissive parent, she'll insist on strict discipline, and will probably be very fortunate in raising her offspring to be independent adults. Her favourite weapons of child psychology are: a wooden paddle, bedtime stories and goodnight kisses.

This woman can be unreasonably temperamental, and create some violent scenes. But her quickly aroused temper will splatter like summer hailstones and soon melt away. She'll never hold a grudge, seek revenge, indulge in self-pity or bitterness. After an emotional storm, her optimistic, April nature will return like the rainbow suddenly appearing after a shower. Lots of people will tell you an Aries woman is completely masculine, but don't you believe them. She's all woman underneath her flashing, forceful exterior, perhaps too much woman for the average man. But, of course, a knight in shining armour isn't an average man. Are there any lonely, courageous knights out there? This is the fair lady of your dreams, worth all the dragons you'll have to slay to win her.

Don't forget that she bruises easily, in spite of her bright, brave smile. (That's just her shield against hurt.) If you can turn the ram into a lamb, you'll have a woman who is honest and passionate, loyal and exciting – though she may be a little impulsive, bossy and independent. Well, you can't have everything, you know. The Aries girl will help you find your lost illusions and she'll have a fierce faith in all your dreams. You don't have any? Borrow some of hers. She has plenty to spare. If you believe in her just half as much as she believes in you, you could make some miracles together.

The Aries Child

'All I know is something comes at me
Like a Jack-in-the-box
And I go up like a Sky Rocket!'

While Papa is passing out the cigars, the crimson-faced little Aries baby will yell for attention in the cradle. How dare you ignore him and talk to the nurse? Who's the boss around here anyway?

You won't any more than get him in the taxi on the way home before that question will be emphatically answered. Your Mars infant is the boss. Do you have any doubts? They'll fade away when he's old enough to sit in the high chair and bang his spoon on the tray if you leave him alone too long. He'll never tease you or be subtle about his preferred diet. There's not a subtle bone in his strong, active, broad-shouldered little body. The Aries tot will spit out his vegetables as if they were shot from a cannon, and rub the cereal bowl on his tiny, bald head to make it quite clear that this is definitely not the food baby likes. The girls will be as direct in their actions as the boys. Maybe more so, though you hardly expect such fierce determination from a soft, little miss. Did I say soft? April's metal is iron, and April's stone is the diamond, the hardest substance known to man.

He'll probably walk earlier than other babies, and certainly will talk earlier. He won't be easy to control. Say, 'No, no,' to an Aries toddler, and he'll shake his chubby, little finger right back at you in defiance. Discipline should be started quite young. Be on guard against falls and injuries to the head or face. He's accident-prone, to put it mildly. Keep sharp knives out of reach, watch out for burns and scalds. If there's anything hot or forbidden around, you can just bet the Aries child will stick his curious fist in it impulsively. You think that will teach him a lesson? Not this youngster. He'll try to break his own record. Teething time may be feverish and severe. Baby will come through the ordeal with little difficulty, but will you?

When he gets a little older, you may get the breath squeezed out of you with one of his loving bear hugs. Aries children are usually affectionately demonstrative, except for the few Mars youngsters whose early emotional experiences freeze their normally warm hearts. These are the sad, quieter little sheep. But their horns are just as dangerous.

Better not ask relatives to babysit without warning them. If poor Aunt Maude bravely takes him while you have a brief vacation, things could become a little strained. She'll catch your Aries tot with his busy hand in the sugar bowl, and probably make the mistake of stamping her foot in displeasure. That will both surprise and outrage the little ram into stamping his own small foot, and bursting out with his first complete sentence, 'Aunt "Mod" – don't you *tell* me sumpin'.' So quaint. Bet she won't 'tell him something' again soon. (You might have to come home a little early. He broke his big toe when he stamped his foot.)

As he grows older and stronger, after having fought measles, mumps, chicken-pox and scarlatina, and won hands down (a battle with germs is no contest with the quickly recuperating Mars nature), your Aries child will begin to show a pattern of temper. You'll notice that he or she can be most unreasonable when thwarted, but the anger won't last long. After a periodic explosion, the Aries boy or girl will beam a large, bright and winning smile your way.

He'll share his toys with amazing generosity with you, his playmates, the postman, the neighbour's bulldog and the alley cat. However, his generosity will end if one of them hurts his feelings or gets in the way of something he wants to do or somewhere he wants to go. Then look out for fireworks.

Aries boys and girls may fall into the early habit of neglecting homework, and using your more obedient little Capricorn, Cancer, Virgo or Pisces child as an example will hardly impress him. (I'm assuming you don't have more than one Aries offspring. The planets don't do that to parents very often.) Instead of shaming the Mars youngster into studying, challenge him. He'll lap up a challenge like that favourite stray alley cat of his laps up cream. Just tell him (or her) that he's probably just slow, or not as bright as the other students, inferior in some way, but you don't mind. You love him anyway. My! How the dust will fly off those schoolbooks, as he sets out to prove what a ridiculous theory *that* is. Someone who can top him? That will be the day – or night.

After you've watched the magic of such strategy at home, tip off his teacher. She'll get down on her knees and thank you. If she has more than one Aries student in her class, she may send you a five-pound box of candy. Actually, Mars youngsters can learn anything in nothing flat, never forget it, and breeze through their studies, if they apply themselves. Not all parents know how to accomplish this. They may spend years wondering why Mike and Maggie test with such a high IQ, and still manage to stay in the third grade for four years. They needn't worry too much, however, because little Mike and Maggie will make up for lost time with the speed of a bullet, once they get out in the world and find out people are smarter than they are. A couple of humiliations to the Mars ego, and they'll cram so fiercely, they'll skip a few grades.

Your April youngster will have a vivid imagination; he'll be as dreamy and sentimental as a storybook, but he'll know very well how to get his bread toasted at the same time. If there is such a contradictory thing as a hard, practical idealistic dreamer, it's your Aries child. He's as naïve as he is tough; as gentle as he is pushy. All these conflicting traits are woven into his fiery little nature. You'll marvel at it and wonder about it. So will your friends later on, not to mention his boss, his future enemies and the unsuspecting soul he marries.

Aries children will take the lead with playmates, start new games and invent new ideas for the gang. They'll insist on having their own way or butt their heads against authority, so you'd better decide to set down some firm rules in the beginning. The Aries child who isn't trained to obey in his youth will be taught some crushing lessons in maturity. Remember that his heart is as soft as butter, and it hides deep-seated fears of being disliked and unloved, despite his brave front. Rejection of his bright dreams or dampening of his exciting enthusiasm, will send him running home to you in tragic tears. Hold him very close when this happens. His heart will be broken. For all his rash domineering ways, the Aries idealism is sensitive and it bruises with the slightest bump. He'll be getting plenty of those bumps on his naïve, hope-filled optimism during his lifetime, and he needs more protection against them than you might think.

He believes in fairy godmothers with magic wands, and giants who can topple over whole cities with one sweep of a powerful hand. Unfortunately, Aries children naïvely identify with these two omnipotent types. When they discover that there are giant killers out there in the brutal world – and blunt realists, who can make those magic wands pathetically impotent, they'll take some hard tumbles. But they'll get back up, brush themselves off, and push forward again indefinitely. *They'll* teach that dull, unimaginative old world a thing or two! There may be a few scars before it's over, but don't count your Mars child out of the fight, no matter how many times he's knocked down. Wait for him to holler 'Uncle'. You may have a long wait.

Hide birthday presents in a safe place. He'll be impatient and unwilling to wait for surprises. Don't destroy his faith in Santa Claus and the Easter Bunny too soon. To first believe fiercely, and then learn not to believe, toughens his emotions. It's a necessary lesson. His allowance will burn a hole right through his pocket, but he'll cheerfully give you his last penny for the milkman. Your Aries daughter may pay the neighbourhood bullies five pence a day to stop stepping on ants. An Aries child handled harshly in the impressionable years can show a defensive cruel streak, but guided gently and wisely, he'll insist on his rights with less force, and show a gigantic generosity and sympathy for his fellow man. Don't give him orders, always ask him to do things with a cheerful smile, and he'll knock himself out to please you. Never destroy his confidence. It's as important to him as the air he breathes. He may run away from home; the

Mars independence shows early, but he'll come back wiser. Teach him that it's unkind to dominate meeker youngsters. He truly does not want to be unkind.

Being around cold, negative people can wound him deeply, but nothing will ever break his spirit. (Remember the diamond.) He'll probably be wild about books and be an excellent reader, yet he may not be anxious to settle down to four years of school. Aries is too interested in getting into the action of chopping down all those challenging beanstalks. But don't give up too quickly. He can use the additional discipline of higher education to help his mind catch up with his flaming emotions and sudden, puzzling bursts of sharp intuition. The more he balks at the idea of a rigid scholastic schedule and prefers the freedom of trying out a few jobs, the more you can be sure he needs the schedule.

He'll have to learn responsibility, but you'll teach him this and other things faster through direct logic and honest affection. Both appeal to him. Parents and teachers should never forget that Aries children glow under praise and doggedly proceed to top their own efforts, but they sputter like firecrackers under attack and lose all incentive to try. Tell him what you like about him, and he'll do less that you don't like. Aries youngsters live up to exactly what's expected of them, including those who hide their burning drive under a calmer personality. This child must always be kept busy, or he'll wander into trouble. Idleness spells danger. He needs stacks of sleep to renew all that scattered, misplaced energy.

He'll love stories about brave, shining heroes, who conquered new worlds. But he also believes in leprechauns and wishing wells, and he'll continue to believe in them long after you've bronzed those little Aries baby shoes and welcomed the first grandchild. If you lead your Mars child gently, with constant love, he'll grow up with the wonderful power to dream the impossible dream – and make it come true.

The Aries Boss

'Well now that we have *seen each other,'* said the Unicorn,
'if you'll believe in me,
I'll believe in you.
Is that a bargain?'

The Aries boss won't be popular with lazy employees. If
you're looking for a temporary soft spot to fill in the time
while you seek a permanent career, or a place to pick up
a little spending money during a lull in your life, you'd
be well advised not to work for an Aries. This man simply
can't abide half-hearted work or a lack of enthusiasm in
those around him. He'll expect you to be as devoted to
the company as he is, and just as intently concerned with
its future potential. He'll probably hire you fast, promote
you fast – and point out your mistakes just as quickly.

If he suspects you are coasting, you're liable to get
a blunt and direct-to-the-point tongue-lashing, with no
feelings spared, but you'll also get a second chance, perhaps even a third or fourth one, if you admit you're wrong
and promise to do better. You might as well be prepared
to work overtime for the Aries boss frequently. He'll
expect it. On the other hand, if he's a typical Aries, he
probably won't frown at the clock or glance at his wrist-
watch when you arrive late in the morning or take an
extra half hour or hour for lunch. He's not a clock watcher
himself. Because of his highly individual personality, he'll
understand that you can't turn on creativity like a light
switch at nine in the morning and turn it off again at five
in the afternoon. He's a boss who will often ask you to

work an extra Saturday, but he's also likely to accept the excuse of your grandmother's funeral when you want to attend that baseball game, though you'd get the time off just as easily by telling the truth. He can see why, on sudden impulse, you'd like to root for your team on a spring day.

Though he'll usually be generous with vacations, salaries, rises and all such matters, he'll fully expect you to drop everything – personal plans, emotional ties, travel commitments or what-have-you – if something of great importance pops up at the office. I hate to say it, but I do know of one Aries boss who had a business crisis requiring the round-the-clock services of a valued employee. The fact that the business emergency occurred on a day this employee was scheduled for an appearance as a bride was incidental. What if she had made plans for six bridesmaids, a flower girl, a ring-bearer, and a reception for three hundred afterwards?

The Aries boss couldn't understand why all that couldn't be postponed, including the honeymoon, for an urgent meeting concerning a million-dollar deal which could put the company on the big board. He would be willing to delay his own marriage for such a crisis, so why wouldn't you? What's the matter, aren't you loyal? This is admittedly an extreme case, but you've been warned.

It's a rare Aries boss who isn't more lavish than the ordinary employer at Christmas time. Depending on how strong an Aries he is, you can count on getting a larger bonus cheque than your friends in other offices – or even a handpicked, expensive gift, which could be something you've been wanting for a long time. A Mars boss is not likely to be stingy (unless there's a conflicting Moon sign or ascendant).

He's not as susceptible to flattery as other astrological signs, but it won't hurt you to pay him a sincere compliment now and then. If you let him know in a straightforward way that you appreciate him as an employer, you admire his efficiency and you think he's just about the smartest boss in town, your job security is guaranteed. However, do or say this only if you really believe it and mean it. He will have contempt for an employee who gurgles his praises just to make points, while he's secretly doubtful of the ram's ability to head the company. The Aries is not ordinarily a good judge of character, but he's so sensitive to other people's opinions of him that he can pretty well tell if he's disliked by those around him day after day. To be liked is his secret need. You might never guess it from his self-confident air and his brave front, but underneath all that swagger he's desperately in need of the approval of his fellow man. That includes you, his wife and his dog – even the stranger in the elevator. Despite that surface independence, nothing makes him happier than to be looked up to and recognized as the capable person he knows he is. On the other hand, nothing can make him as depressed, cranky and sometimes downright petty as suspecting that those who work for him don't approve of his methods or don't realize his value and potential.

If you hear a rumour that the company is about to go bankrupt, don't look around for another job too quickly. You may not need a new job, after all. If anybody can pull the company out of trouble, save it at the last minute from financial disaster under the most dire circumstances, and make the entire operation seem rather like Moses parting the Red Sea, it's your Aries boss. He's independent, daring and venturesome. His drive (unlike the more emotional drive of the Scorpio) is vital, from the spirit, and almost always idealistic. (He may lose out to the equally determined Scorpio pitted against him, however, and be unable to match the steady ruthlessness of Pluto – though he'll recover from the loss and win somewhere else.)

Aries initiates. If there's a suggestion box around the office and you drop in enough workable, creative ideas, you're almost sure to advance to a high position quickly with this man. He appreciates employees who care enough about the company to make suggestions and who are original in their thinking – as long as they make it perfectly clear they have no intentions of trying to outshine him.

Will-power is one of the strong features of the Aries man. He fights off all minor ailments and he won't give in to serious illness either. Sometimes he can delay or entirely prevent disease by sheer positive thinking. If he does have a cold or virus infection (probably accompanied by a high fever), he'll get dressed to come in to the office for some urgent business and by the time he arrives, the fever may be gone, to the mystification of his doctor and the suspicion of his employees that he was really at home goofing off.

The Mars will is so fantastically strong that your Aries boss (who will probably be fairly lucky at gambling) can go to the racetrack and practically root his horse into the lead. You're bound to feel the effect of such a forceful personality, so expect plenty of fireworks, excitement, chaos and intense activity around the office. Your business day will seldom be uneventful. Something will always be happening.

There will be nothing lethargic about him, and there had better not be anything lethargic about you. Your

Aries employer will probably have little interest in any previous bad job record you held before or in the reasons why your former boss may have fired you. He's the best bet to approach under these circumstances. Because of his conviction that he's going to make the future what he wants it to be, Aries is seldom bothered or concerned by the past. Yours or his.

The Mars executive is too proud to let others know they've hurt him. In spite of quick outbursts of temper (which won't last long or be vindictive, and will be forgotten as soon as they're over), he will hide quite well those things which truly affect him deeply. The ram won't admit his dependence on anyone but himself. He does need others – far more than he will ever admit, but his strength comes from inside, and he can always find a way of going it alone when he must.

If you can admire his energy and courage, though you find it impossible to imitate; if you can make up for his impulsive, slapdash ways by patiently filling in the details he's overlooked in his haste (and do this unobtrusively), he'll probably pay you more money than you can make anywhere else and you'll be with him for life. Tactfully attempt to keep him from doing or saying rash things he'll regret later. Remind him gently that those to whom he directs his temporary righteous anger may be Very Important People and they could react in a way which will hurt his business if he alienates them.

That's the important thing to remember about your Aries boss. In spite of his great independent spirit, when his idealistic, optimistic enthusiasm gets him in over his head, he really needs your help, faith and loyalty. Give these to him in abundance and you'll never find a pink slip in your pay envelope. You won't have to worry when missing a taxi in rainy weather makes you late for work, if you need an extra week's vacation time for an operation – or about someone younger and more efficient replacing you. More than any other kind of boss, he'll repay loyalty with loyalty. Keep a full supply of aspirin in the desk drawer for frequent emergencies, polish up your smile, don't take his outbursts seriously – and you can throw away the classified ads. You'll want to stay where the action is.

The Aries Employee

'I said it very loud and clear
I went and shouted in his ear
And when I found the door was locked
I pulled and pushed and kicked and knocked . . .'

'But it's no use going back to yesterday
Because I was a different person then.'

A job interview with a prospective Aries employee, if he's a typical ram, might run something like this:

EMPLOYER: I see from your resumé and references that you've been with six different firms in the past two years, Mr Bootsikaris.

ARIES: Call me Charlie, Mr Flaxman. Yes, I believe in trying to advance myself. When you outgrow a job, what's the point of staying in a position where there's nothing more you can learn and nothing more you can contribute to the company?

EMPLOYER: That's just what bothers me Char – uh, Mr Bootsikaris. I'm afraid you may outgrow us in a short time, also, after we've spent the money to train you.

ARIES: I thought that might concern you. But you don't have to worry. I've investigated your company, and I'm sure I wouldn't feel restless, because I can see there's plenty of opportunity with you for anyone who really tries.

I've always wanted to work with a really great, creative and progressive management. They're so rare that I'd rather wait till there's an opening here than go anywhere else.

Needless to say, the boss who can overcome his initial shock at such an unusual interview is likely to hire the Aries on the spot. That kind of sincere enthusiasm for the company is hard to come by in these days of security-minded and union-conscious employees – never mind the abruptness and the superego.

Hiring an Aries can be the smartest move you ever made or the largest headache you've ever known, depending on how you aim this combustible, misguided missile. Aiming him towards a routine, nine-to-five job is the wrong direction. In the beginning, he may shine like a silver dollar to impress you, but it won't be long before he's restless and unhappy. And he'll let you know it in unmistakable ways, like coming in a little later each day, taking extra time for lunch, or writing personal letters at his desk. These are all danger signals that your Aries employee is not satisfied. He's still extremely valuable to your firm, but he's bored, and when the ram gets bored, his virtues are quickly buried under his shortcomings.

Put your Aries worker in a position where he has complete freedom to make decisions, answerable, if possible, only to you. If you can do it without hurting office morale, allow him to come to work at odd hours. After a short period you'll notice that, although he may appear as late as ten or eleven in the morning, or take two hours for lunch, he'll also be the very last one to leave at night, especially if there's extra work to get out. He's more likely

than any of your other employees to accept additional
assignments as a challenge, without complaining.

Many an Aries will labour until the wee small hours,
if it's necessary, or if there's an exciting project under
way, and probably be more familiar to the nightly clean-
ing woman than to the early morning switchboard recep-
tionist. You won't find him getting edgy or peeking at the
clock around five o'clock, so why should you be fussy if
it's twenty minutes past ten when he arrives in the morning? That's his reasoning, and there's a certain logic
in it.

The Arian is constitutionally unable to keep to a tight
and uniform schedule, regardless of standard office pro-
cedure. His great, creative energy comes on him at all
hours, and it can't be adjusted to fit someone's idea of
the proper working day. He may ask to leave early some
afternoon for pressing personal reasons, but he'll come
back later the same night to burn the midnight oil, or pop
in before the birdies chirp the following morning to make
up the work he's missed. One thing Aries can't stand is
to turn in work which is less perfect than he knows he
can do. Despite his carelessness with detail and his disdain
of normal office routine, that quality is too good to miss.
It's worth putting up with the Mars independence to
take advantage of his wonderful determination to succeed,
which will obviously benefit your company, if you're
astute enough and patient enough to utilize it properly.

Money is never his prime reason for working. He will
insist on being paid what he's worth (what *he* thinks he's
worth) for the sake of ego and status, but money is never
his main objective. He's motivated by success, and cash
is always secondary. He may frequently ask to borrow
money, because the ram usually lives beyond his income.

Still, an extra pat on the back will often get more out of him than an extra five dollars a week in his pay envelope. Of course, you may have to tame his natural desire to take over everyone else's department, since he's bursting with ideas of how everyone in the firm could get where they're going faster, including you. But if you can learn not to take offence at his frequent and impertinent suggestions, you'll find a bonus of original and profitable thoughts.

Always put Aries in the action job, in a position where he can get out and promote the firm and mix with people. Never put him behind a desk where he has to do the same thing day after day under the scrutiny of another employee. Aries will take orders willingly from very few people, since he believes very few people are superior to him. He undoubtedly thinks you are, or he wouldn't have got mixed up with you in the first place. Once he's sure you understand and appreciate his efforts, he'll probably be the most loyal, hard-working and competent employee on your payroll. But put him in an inferior position and he'll be reluctant to make any but the most perfunctory effort.

Naturally, he can't always start at the top, though he'd like to. If he must begin at the bottom and learn a new trade or profession, try to add some kind of important-sounding responsibility to his daily duties, so he'll at least think he's at the top. It allows him to save face with himself. To bring out his best, he needs to feel that the place couldn't run without him. The ram is a natural promoter. He'll promote your business to his wife and friends enthusiastically, to cab drivers, waiters and anyone else who will listen – at the movies, in the swimming pool – and not just during the hours he's being paid to do so.

He'll turn everyone from his broker to his insurance man into a booster for your firm. Few people (except Leos) can equal him in bringing in new accounts, saving customers you thought were hopelessly lost and putting over the largest, most ambitious schemes you can devise – especially when he thinks you're depending on him to come through.

If there's ever any kind of financial trouble, your Aries employee is not one to desert a sinking ship. He'll stick with you through the crisis, and possibly add a few ideas of his own about how to solve it. The Arian is literally unable to conceive that anything or anyone he believes in, including himself, can fail. Obviously, such a trait can be mighty welcome some black day.

Ask this employee to work over weekends or holidays, take a temporary cut in salary during an emergency or perform someone else's job in addition to his own in case of illness or vacation, and he'll seldom complain. Just be sure you thank him warmly and let him know you honestly appreciate it. There's little he won't do to get enthusiastic approval from you. Never give someone else credit for work he's done, never make him feel guilty about being late, don't compliment others too often when he's around, don't harp on his mistakes – especially in front of other people – and never give him the impression you wish he'd stay in his place. Otherwise, he'll be irritable, frustrated and lazy. You won't have to fire him. He'll most likely quit before you get around to it. It's usually not necessary to scold the ram, anyway. He'll be the first to apologize for errors he's committed through his natural haste and impulsiveness, if he's met halfway, and he'll sincerely try not to repeat them. Even if he's not always successful in that attempt, his intentions are admirable. You may want to train him tactfully and privately not to be so rash and over-confident, but never break his spirit. If you try, you'll fail, and the attempts will just lose you all that refreshing and valuable optimism.

When you recognize his talents, Aries will literally knock himself out to top himself. Criticism will never accomplish its intended purpose with him. Besides, he's more often right than wrong with his hunches, no matter what some of the experts who have been around for years might think. Aries has an uncanny ability to understand today with a clarity not possessed either by those who cling to yesterday or those who pin all their hopes on tomorrow. So it pays to listen to him, even though his eagerness and his sureness that he's right makes him drop his manners now and then, with a loud and unpleasant thud.

As soon as you can, give him a rise or a title to let him know he's doing well and that you're pleased, and by all means, as quickly as you can, let him either work alone, or lead others. Let him feel he's your personal associate. It's imperative that those dealing with an Aries in any working or professional capacity realize that he will pour out an amazing number of valuable contributions to the project at hand only if he feels that, in some way, he's important. When his excitement and his idealism are dampened, he quickly loses interest, becomes disheartened and stands back to let others take over – glum and miserable – an unnecessary waste of rare and useful talent. Unless the ram is allowed to promote, create and originate, he's no use to himself or anyone else. Logic and kindness will reach him every time.

Because he's a natural innovator and leader, Aries is at home in almost any career or profession. There are no special places where he thrives best. Whether it's a greenhouse or a police station – whether he wears a fireman's hat or a surgeon's mask – he must be in charge. The fields of advertising and public relations attract him, since they give him a chance to promote, and he takes to selling like a duck takes to water. But you can place him in any job, from teaching to lorry-driving – from broadcasting to building – and he'll fit right into the slot, if the slot is wide enough to take up his excess energy and ego.

You may run across a ram who hides his drive under a calmer, more controlled manner, but don't kid yourself into thinking you can push him into the corner. That's for little Jack Horner, not him. His place is in front – avant-garde. Channel his abilities and he'll make a heap of money for you, as well as giving you unswerving, unquestioned loyalty – especially when the chips are down. If you do a little comparative shopping around, you'll find those virtues are invaluable.

Afterword

How many miles to Babylon?
Three-score-miles-and-ten.
Can I get there by candlelight?
Yes – and back again!
Mother Goose

Shake her snow-white feathers, tune in to her nonsensical wavelength, and old Mother Goose may show us a secret message. There may be a pearl of wisdom hidden in the apparently childish prattle of her nursery rhyme.

How many miles to Babylon? It seems to be quite a leap from the sandal-clad people of Chaldea and the jewelled, perfumed Pharaohs of Egypt to the space age – from the lost continent of Atlantis to the jet-propelled Twentieth Century. But how far is it, really? Perhaps only a dream or two.

Alone among the sciences, astrology has spanned the centuries and made the journey intact. We shouldn't be surprised that it remains with us, unchanged by time – because astrology is truth – and truth is eternal. Echoing the men and women of the earliest known civilizations, today's moderns repeat identical phrases: 'Is Venus your ruling planet?' 'I was born when the Sun was in Taurus.' 'Is your Mercury in Gemini too?' 'Wouldn't you just know he's an Aquarian?'

Astrological language is a golden cord that binds us to a dim past while it prepares us for an exciting future of planetary explorations. Breathtaking Buck Rogers advances in all fields of science are reminding us that 'there are more things in heaven and earth, Horatio, than are dreamt of in your philosophy' (even if your name is Sam or Fanny instead of Horatio). Dick Tracy's two-way wrist radio is no longer a fantastic dream – it's reality – and Moon Maid's powerful weapon has been matched by the miracle of the laser beam, the highly concentrated light that makes lead run like water and penetrates the hardest substances known to man. Jules Verne and Flash Gordon are now considered pretty groovy prophets, so there were obviously important secrets buried in those way-out adventures twenty thousand leagues under the sea and many trillions of leagues above the earth.

Could it be that the science-fiction writers and cartoonists have a better idea of the true distance between yesterday, today and tomorrow than the white-coated men in their sterile, chrome laboratories? Einstein knew that time was only relative. The poets have always been aware – and the wise men, down through the ages. The message is not new. Long before today's overwhelming interest in astrology, daring men of vision like Plato, Ptolemy, Hippocrates and Columbus respected its wisdom; and they've been kept good company by the likes of Galileo, Ben Franklin, Thomas Jefferson, Sir Isaac Newton and Dr Carl Jung. You can add President John Quincy Adams to the list; also great astronomers like Tycho Brahe, Johannes Kepler and Dr Gustave Stromberg. And don't forget RCA's brilliant research scientist, John Nelson, famed mathematician, Dr Kuno Foelsch and Pulitzer prize winner, John O'Neill. None of these men were high school drop-outs.

In 1953, Dr Frank A. Brown, Jr, of North-western University, made a startling discovery while he was experimenting with some oysters. Science has always assumed that oysters open and close with the cycle of the tides of their birthplace. But when Dr Brown's oysters were taken from the waters of Long Island Sound and placed in a tank of water in his Evanston, Illinois laboratory, a strange pattern emerged.

Their new home was kept at an even temperature, and the room was illuminated with a steady, dim light. For two weeks, the displaced oysters opened and closed their shells with the same rhythm as the tides of Long Island Sound – one thousand miles away. Then they suddenly snapped shut, and remained that way for several hours. Just as Dr Brown and his research team were about to consider the case of the homesick oysters closed, an odd thing happened. The shells opened wide once again. Exactly four hours after the high tide at Long Island Sound – at the precise moment when there would have been a high tide at Evanston, Illinois, if it were on the sea coast – a new cycle began. They were adapting their rhythm to the new geographical latitude and longitude. By what force? By the moon, of course. Dr Brown had to conclude that the oysters' energy cycles are ruled by the mysterious lunar signal that controls the tides.

Human energy and emotional cycles are governed by the same kind of planetary forces, in a much more complicated network of magnetic impulses from all the planets. Science recognizes the moon's power to move great bodies of water. Since man himself consists of seventy per cent water, why should he be immune to such forceful planetary pulls? The tremendous effects of magnetic gravity on orbiting astronauts as they get closer to the planets is well known. What about the proven correlation between lunar motion and women's cycles, including childbirth – and the repeated testimony of doctors and nurses in the wards of mental hospitals, who are only too familiar with the influence of the moon's changes on their patients? Did you ever talk to a policeman who had to work a rough beat on the night of a full moon? Try to find a farmer who will sink a fence rail, slaughter a pig or plant crops without astrological advice from his trusted *Farmer's Almanac*. The movements of the moon and the planets are as important to him as the latest farm bill controversy in Congress.

Of all the heavenly bodies, the Moon's power is more visible and dramatic, simply because it's the closest body to the earth. But the Sun, Venus, Mars, Mercury, Jupiter, Saturn, Uranus, Neptune and Pluto exercise their influences just as surely, even though from farther away. Scientists are aware that plants and animals are influenced by cycles at regular intervals, and that the cycles are governed through forces such as electricity in the air, fluctuations in barometric pressure and the gravitational field. These earthly forces are originally triggered by magnetic vibrations from outer space, where the planets live, and from where they send forth their unseen waves. Phases of the moon, showers of gamma rays, cosmic rays, X-rays, undulations of the pear-shaped electromagnetic field and other influences from extraterrestrial sources are constantly penetrating and bombarding the atmosphere around us. No living organism escapes it, nor do the minerals. Nor do we.

Dr Harold S. Burr, emeritus Professor of Anatomy at Yale's Medical School, states that a complex magnetic field not only establishes the pattern of the human brain at birth, but continues to regulate and control it through life. He further states that the human central nervous system is a superb receptor of electromagnetic energies, the finest in nature. (We may walk with a fancier step, but we hear the same drummer as the oysters.) The ten million cells in our brains form a myriad of possible circuits through which electricity can channel.

Therefore, the mineral and chemical content and the electrical cells of our bodies and brains respond to the magnetic influence of every sunspot, eclipse and planetary movement. We are synchronized, like all other living organisms, metals and minerals, to the ceaseless ebb and flow of the universe; but we need not be imprisoned by it, because of our own free will. The soul, in other words, is superior to the power of the planets. Yet unfortunately, most of us fail to use our free will (i.e., the power of the soul), and are just about as helpless to control our destinies as Lake Michigan or an ear of corn. The purpose of the astrologer is to help us gain the knowledge of how to avoid drifting downstream – how to fight the current.

Astrology is an art as well as a science. Though lots of people would like to ignore that basic fact, it can't be overlooked. There are astrologers who tremble with anger at the mere mention of intuition in relation to astrology. They send out fiery blasts against any hint of such a correlation, and frantically insist that 'Astrology is an exact science, based on mathematics. It should never be mentioned in the same breath with intuitive powers.' I regard their opinions as sincere, but logic forces me to ask why these must be so totally separate. Should they be? Even the layman today is attempting, through books, games and parlour or laboratory testing, to determine his or her ESP potential. Why not astrologers? Are they supposed to bury their heads in the sand like ostriches concerning the development of a sixth sense, or the existence of it in some individuals?

Granted, the calculation of an astrological chart, based on mathematical data and astronomical facts, is an exact science. But medicine is also science, based on fact and research. Yet, all good doctors admit that medicine is an art as well. The intuitive diagnostician is recognized by his colleagues. Physicians will tell you that they each have, in varying degrees, a certain sensitivity, which is an invaluable aid in interpreting the provable facts of medicine. To synthesize medical theories, to interpret the results of laboratory tests in relation to the patient's individual history, is never cut and dried. It simply couldn't be done without intuitive perception on the part of the doctor. Otherwise, medicine could simply be computerized.

Music is also scientifically based – on the inflexible law of mathematics – as everyone who has ever studied chord progressions knows. Musical interludes are governed by ratios of whole numbers – a science, indisputably – it's also an art. Anyone can be taught to play *Clair de lune* or *The Warsaw Concerto* correctly but it's the sensitivity or intuitive perception of a Van Cliburn that separates him from the rest of us. The notes and chords are always the same, mathematically exact. The interpretation, however, is different – an obvious reality which has nothing to do with present definition of the word science.

Many intelligent people can study or teach astrology successfully, even brilliantly, but few are able to add the dimension of sensitive interpretation or intuitive perception that makes the science of astrology ultimately satisfying as an art. Of course, one doesn't have to be a psychic or a medium to give an accurate and helpful astrological analysis, yet any intuition on the part of the astrologer is clearly an asset to his synthesis of the natal chart. Naturally, the intuitive astrologer must also be well versed in mathematical calculation and must strictly observe the scientific fundamentals of his art. Assuming he is and does, he's using a powerful combination of both conscious and subconscious abilities, so you needn't be frightened into avoiding competent professionals who are able to make both an art and a science of their work. If anything, you'll be lucky to find one. Sensitive perception is rare in any field.

The popularity of astrology today is bringing all the quacks out of the woodwork, and there aren't as many qualified astrologers and teachers as there should be. Possibly within the next decade, astrologers will be recognized professionals, who have graduated from an 'astral science' course in a leading college. The important study of the influence of the planets on human behaviour will be then taught in the modern halls of ivy, as it was once taught in the great universities of Europe. Students will be accepted only if their natal charts reveal an ability to teach or research in astrology or to give a personal analysis; and the courses will be as tough as those in any law or medical school. The subjects of magnetic weather conditions, biology, chemistry, geology, astronomy, higher mathematics, sociology, comparative religions, philosophy and psychology will be required – as well as instruction in calculating an astrological chart and interpreting it – and graduates will proudly set up a plaque reading: 'John Smith – Astrologer, DAS' (Doctor of Astral Science).

At the present stage of research and acceptance, the safest and sanest approach to astrology by the layman is to become thoroughly acquainted with the twelve signs, which is on a par with becoming acquainted with the theories of medicine by studying first aid or sensible health rules.

Mankind will some day discover that astrology, medicine, religion, astronomy and psychiatry are all one. When they are blended, each will be whole. Until then, each will be slightly defective.

There is an area of confusion in astrology about which opinions clash. Reincarnation. There's not a person today who doesn't have either a positive or a negative approach to the law of karma. You can't avoid learning and reading about it any more than you can avoid exposure to the ouija board under the Uranus influence of this Twentieth-Century movement into the Aquarian age.

Esoteric astrologers believe, as I do, that astrology is incomplete unless properly interpreted with the law of karma as its foundation. There are others who emphatically deny this, especially in the western world, to which astrology is comparatively new. You needn't accept reincarnation to derive benefit from astrology; and the proof of the soul's existence in previous lives, however logical, has never been scientifically established (though some mighty convincing circumstantial evidence is available, including documented cases and the Bible itself). Because of its very nature, reincarnation may for ever elude absolute, tangible proof. The ancients taught that the evolved soul must reach the point of seeking the truth of karma, in order to end the cycle of rebirth. Therefore, faith in reincarnation is a gift – a reward for the soul advanced enough to search for the meaning of its existence in the universe and its karmic obligations in the present life. Proof of this deep mystery would remove the individual free will of discovery, so perhaps man must always look for the answers to reincarnation in his own heart.

But he should do so only after intelligent study of what other minds have found to be both false and true. Books written about the amazing prophet Edgar Cayce will give the curious layman a better understanding of what it's all about, and there are many other excellent works on the market concerning reincarnation, which will help you establish for yourself whether the subject is worthy of your consideration or just so much black magic. That's the only way to approach such a personal matter as life and death – by yourself – after a thorough examination of the pros and cons.

We are heading in the direction of new respect for unseen influences, and the current interest in mental telepathy is a good example. Huge sums of money have been and are being spent by NASA in ESP tests with selected astronauts to determine the possibility of transferring mental messages through sense perception, as an emergency measure against a breakdown of present communications between earth and astronaut. Russia is rumoured to be far ahead of us in this area of research, another reason why dogmatic, materialistic thinking must go.

The excitement of distinguished scientists about experiments with these invisible wavelengths between human minds has gained the attention of the medical doctors. Medicine has long admitted that such ailments as ulcers and strep throat are brought on by mental strain, or emotional tension, and now physicians are advancing serious theories that there is a definite relationship between the personality of the patient and the growth and development of cancer. Recent articles by well-known doctors have urged the co-operation of psychiatrists in determining in advance which patient may be susceptible, so the disease can be treated early or even prevented. Yet

astrology has always known that disease is triggered by
the mind and emotions, and can be controlled or elimin-
ated the same way; also that people born under certain
planetary influences are either susceptible or immune to
particular diseases and accidents. The knowledge medicine seeks is in the patient's carefully calculated, detailed
natal chart, clearly shown by his planetary positions and
aspects at birth.

The astrologer–physicians in ancient Egypt practised
brain surgery with refined techniques, a fact recently
proven by archaeological and anthropological discoveries.
Today's progressive doctors are quietly checking the
astrological sign the moon is transiting before surgery,
imitating the Greek physicians of centuries ago, who followed Hippocrates' precept of: 'Touch not with metal
that part of the anatomy ruled by the sign the Moon is
transiting, or to which the transiting Moon is in square
or opposition by aspect.' There's much that's compelling
and important to say about medical astrology and its
value to the physician in the cause and prevention of
illness, but it's such a huge subject, it must wait for
another volume.

Moving from medicine to travel, several insurance com-
panies and airlines are secretly investigating the possible
relationship between fatal plane crashes and the natal
charts of the passengers and crew. So time marches on –
from ancient knowledge of planetary influences – retro-
grading back to materialistic thinking – and forward again
to truth. Down through the centuries the planets remain
unchanged in their grandeur and their orbs. The stars
which shone over Babylon and the stable in Bethlehem
still shine as brightly over the Empire State Building and
your front garden today. They perform their cycles with

the same mathematical precision, and they will continue to affect each thing on earth, including man, as long as the earth exists.

Always remember that astrology is not fatalistic. The stars incline, they do not compel. Most of us are carried along in blind obedience to the influence of the planets and our electromagnetic birth patterns, as well as to our environment, our heredity and the wills of those stronger than us. We show no perception, therefore no resistance; and our horoscopes fit us like a fingerprint. We're moved like pawns on a chess-board in the game of life, even while some of us scoff at or ignore the very powers which are moving us. But anyone can rise above the afflictions of his nativity. By using free will, or the powers of the soul, anyone can dominate his moods, change his character, control his environment and the attitudes of those close to him. When we do this, we become movers in the chess game, instead of the pawns.

Do you refrain from following your star by saying, 'I just wasn't born with the strength or the ability'? You were born with more of each than Helen Keller, who called on the deep, inner power of her will to overcome being blind, deaf and dumb. She replaced these natal afflictions with fame, wealth, respect and the love of thousands, and she conquered her planetary influences.

Do constant fears keep you from seeing tomorrow? Do melancholy and pessimism colour your rainbows grey before you even reach out to touch them? Actress Patricia Neal substituted iron nerve for gloomy apprehension. She smiled at tragedy, and her grin gave her enough emotional energy to astound her doctors by literally forcing the paralysis of a near-fatal stroke to vaporize.

Do newspaper headlines have you convinced America

is doomed to oblivion in the near future, through the stalemate of hot and cold wars, lack of national and international understanding, rising crime rates, injustice, prejudice, moral decadence, loss of ethics and the possibility of nuclear destruction? Winston Churchill once faced certain defeat for himself personally – and for his country. But he put a twinkle in his eyes, a piece of steel in his spine and a prayer in his heart. That triple combination wrought a miracle, as the courage of one man aroused thousands to blind optimism and stubborn strength. The resulting magnetic vibrations melted the lead of fear, inspired the world and made victory the prize. He refused to be a pawn of the planets or let his country be the pawn of their influence.

You say such people are special? But these could be your miracles. All of them. There's enough magnetic power in you to make you immune to the strongest planetary pulls, now or in the future. What a pity to submit so easily and let your potential remain unrealized.

When both hate and fear are conquered, the will is then free and capable of immense power. This is the message of your own nativity, hidden in the silent stars. Listen to it.

An ancient legend tells of a man who went to a wise mystic to ask for the key to power and occult secrets. He was taken to the edge of a clear lake, and told to kneel down. Then the wise one disappeared, and the man was left alone, staring down at his own reflected image in the water.

'What I do, you can do also.' 'Ask, and you shall receive.' 'Knock, and it shall be opened unto you.' 'Seek the truth, and the truth shall set you free.'

'How many miles to Babylon? Three-score-miles-and-

ten. Can I get there by candlelight? Yes – and back again!'
Is it a poem, or is it a riddle? Each thing in the universe
is part of the universal law, and astrology is the basis of
that law. Out of astrology grew religion, medicine and
astronomy, not the other way round.

There's a sculptured zodiac in the temple of Thebes,
so old that its origin has never been determined. Atlantis?
Perhaps. But wherever it's from and whoever carved its
symbols, its message is eternal: you are endless galaxies
– and you have seen but one star.

Linda Goodman
Linda Goodman's Love Signs £6.99

A new approach to the human heart and personal relationships. A compulsively readable book exploring the tensions and harmony inherent in your associations with people born under the same sun signs as yourself, or under the other eleven signs. Also features: in-depth exploration of the seventy-eight sun sign patterns for both sexes; lists of famous people under your sign; explanations of the twelve mysteries of love.

Linda Goodman's Sun Signs £4.99

Have you ever wondered about yourself? What you are really like, whether you'll make a good wife, mother or lover, whether other people like you? Linda Goodman reveals the real you, your personality and character as the stars see you, in this remarkably lively and down-to-earth book.

All Pan books are available at your local bookshop or newsagent, or can be ordered direct from the publisher. Indicate the number of copies required and fill in the form below.

Send to: **CS Department, Pan Books Ltd., P.O. Box 40, Basingstoke, Hants. RG21 2YT.**

or phone: 0256 469551 (Ansaphone), quoting title, author and Credit Card number.

Please enclose a remittance* to the value of the cover price plus: 60p for the first book plus 30p per copy for each additional book ordered to a maximum charge of £2.40 to cover postage and packing.

*Payment may be made in sterling by UK personal cheque, postal order, sterling draft or international money order, made payable to Pan Books Ltd.

Alternatively by Barclaycard/Access:

Card No.

Signature:

Applicable only in the UK and Republic of Ireland.

While every effort is made to keep prices low, it is sometimes necessary to increase prices at short notice. Pan Books reserve the right to show on covers and charge new retail prices which may differ from those advertised in the text or elsewhere.

NAME AND ADDRESS IN BLOCK LETTERS PLEASE:

....

Name ——————————————————————

Address ——————————————————————

——————————————————————

——————————————————————

——————————————————————

3/87